COHERENT LEADERSHIP

Prosperity and Purpose in All Aspects of Life

LARA BEZERRA

Coherent Leadership: Prosperity and Purpose in All Aspects of Life

Printed in the United States of America

Hardcover ISBN: 978-1-965253-86-1
Paperback ISBN: 978-1-965253-87-8
Ebook ISBN: 978-1-965253-88-5
Library of Congress Control Number: 2026912026

DartFrog

DartFrog Books, LLC.
www.DartFrogBooks.com

TABLE OF CONTENTS

This book is dedicated to everyone who believes in humanity and our capacity to evolve and lead from the heart. And to those who understand that consciousness is not abstract but a practical choice—expressed in how we think, decide, relate, and take responsibility for the systems we influence.

INTRODUCTION

I have always believed in human beings, perhaps even more than they believe in themselves. Since I was young, I've felt that people carry an extraordinary potential inside them—an exponential capacity to grow, to love, to create, and to make life beautiful. And I haven't become cynical with age. The more I've lived, the more I've witnessed the infinite possibility that exists when human beings discover their purpose and align their lives with it.

And even more powerful is what I've seen when we align our purposes together. When we're motivated by love, by meaning, by something bigger than personal success, something extraordinary happens: wisdom emerges, relationships strengthen, decisions become clearer, and collective prosperity flourishes. I've watched this unfold in families, in teams, in organizations, and in entire communities. It's one of the most beautiful expressions of humanity I know. And it's the reason I care so deeply about writing this book.

My understanding of people, purpose, and coherence wasn't born from theories or leadership manuals. It was shaped by life. I was raised in a family that taught me to see beauty even in difficulty, and later I was shaped by leadership roles that demanded humility, courage, and deep reflection. In 2003, I found myself leading a multinational company in Hungary, a foreigner, not speaking the language, not knowing the market. In my early thirties, I was the youngest member of my leadership team, and my ego wanted me to prove myself, but life wanted to teach me trust. Hungary had just been accepted to the European Union, and our industry was being forced to reform its practices to meet new European regulations, but before we could rebuild our industry's reputation, we had to rebuild trust among ourselves as an organization. Only by doing that could we support the transformation our industry needed. That meant the people I was leading had to start trusting me and I had to trust myself, my purpose, and the intention behind my leadership. And so *bizalom*—trust —became my guide.

Looking back years later, I understood why this journey worked: because every transformation started inside, not outside. We became coherent—individually and collectively—and as soon as we did, everything around us began to change. Leadership stopped being about performance and started being about helping human beings to flourish. My teams grew, my organizations evolved, and I grew with them. We created systems that resonated with purpose instead of fear. We built environments where people felt trusted, seen, and capable of becoming better versions of themselves. We created coherence.

At the same time, my personal life deepened my contemplative practices: yoga, meditation, spirituality, and constant learning. Building a family, losing my mother, and facing moments of profound questioning pushed me to connect science, spirituality, and lived experience. Through all of it, one truth became clear: Our purpose is the frame through which life makes sense. When we act from that frame, even life's hardest challenges become part of our growth. They stop being obstacles and become training fields for the soul.

This book is my attempt to translate everything I've lived, learned, researched, and observed into a guide that supports you—whoever you are, wherever you are in your journey—as you pursue the coherent life. I don't write because I have all the answers; I write because I've lived the questions deeply. I've witnessed what coherence can do in families, in teams, in multinational organizations, and in myself. And I believe this awareness can help you transform your life too.

My hopes for you are simple and profound:

That you will rediscover your own capacity to contemplate, to be intentional, to act with clarity, and to live with **integrality,** aware of every system that shapes your life.

That you will understand the invisible patterns—emotional, relational, biological, and systemic—that influence your decisions.

That you will gain the courage to align who you are with how you live, embracing difficulties as a training field for becoming more resilient and enjoying life even in its downturns.

And that you will experience the beauty of coherence, not as a concept but as a way of being.

In these pages, we'll explore four essential pillars of coherence: **integrality**, **intentionality**, **coherence as practice,** and **lifelong learning.** We'll reflect on how dissonance arises, how resonance amplifies collective potential, how systems shape our lives, and how purpose guides us toward wiser choices and deeper fulfillment.

This book is an invitation—not to follow my way but to find your own, consciously and coherently. My wish is that as you finish reading, you will feel more connected to yourself, more aligned with your purpose, and more capable of shaping a future that's bright, harmonic, and meaningful.

Let's walk this journey together.

PART ONE

THE POWER OF COHERENT LIVING AND LEADING

CHAPTER 1

COHERENCE CHANGES LIVES—OURS AND OTHERS'

When Paul Clay contacted me, he was concerned about the conflict he and his brothers were experiencing. He didn't know if it was about the company they'd inherited or some misunderstanding that had set in since their father's passing. They wanted to continue their father's legacy of having a positive impact on their communities and their country, but Paul had recently found out that his brothers weren't pleased with some of his decisions as CEO. For example, he'd sold a manufacturing plant that wasn't especially profitable but had a sentimental value for their family, as it was part of their father's legacy. Although he had the future of the company in mind, these kinds of autonomous decisions were making relations among the brothers increasingly uncomfortable. They even considered selling the company to preserve their relationships. And there was more. Paul discovered that his brothers had been unhappy for some time about other issues as well but hadn't said anything because they were afraid of risking their fragile relationships—an all-too-common dynamic in family businesses.

Instead of authentically engaging and resolving their misunderstandings, the Clay brothers resigned themselves to having merely cordial relationships, but their effort to avoid hurting each other had backfired. Rather than preserving their family bonds, it strained and weakened them. If they were going to restore their close bonds and run their company successfully, they had to become aware of their dissonance and get back in sync with each other.

My work with them began with a workshop to restore their connection and introduce new concepts for them to work with, and some mentoring sessions to reinforce that work. Their relationships began to shift from dissonance to resonance. To have any hope of recovering close personal relationships that are in jeopardy and leading a successful company, this shift is absolutely essential.

Dissonance Destroys

Dissonance is a lack of alignment between what we collectively pursue and what we individually want. When people work together in pursuit of an objective, their inner desires should be on the table, and the final goal should be aligned with their individual purposes even if those purposes are different from each other. When some of the parties involved say they're okay with the goals agreed upon but their individual desires lie in a different direction, this causes dissonance and is one of the biggest obstacles to achieving a collective goal.

Dissonance divides us and impedes our progress. When people disagree or have split opinions, the conversation turns into a debate and sometimes an argument, but at least their opinions are out there. Then the task becomes to learn to disagree better. But as in the Clay family, when people feel they can't express their opinions and they assume the worst about what isn't being said, there will be dissonance until the matter is settled. In the meantime, productivity will drop, and if the situation goes on for too long, relationships may be damaged irreparably. And considering that the brothers were Generation Xers, it would serve them to work things out sooner rather than later. They still had long careers ahead of them, and the longer they took to resolve the situation, the more they had to lose.

When two vibrating systems have frequencies that don't align well, they will partially cancel each other out. In quantum mechanics, this phenomenon is called destructive interference. Imagine two waves rolling away from the shore. If the crest (peak) of one wave meets the trough (valley) of the other, they minimize each other, resulting in a smaller, weaker, less visible wave, and sometimes no wave at all. But if the crests of the waves merge, they create a larger, stronger, more visible wave. This is called **constructive interference.** If we look at resonance through the lens of quantum physics, we find a powerful metaphor for human connection. Resonance waves occur when a sound or light wave strikes an object that's already vibrating at a particular frequency. If the frequencies match, the object begins to vibrate more strongly. And the same happens in human relationships: When people are aligned in intention and constructive motivation they amplify each other's energy. Like quantum resonance, this shared frequency doesn't just add; it multiplies. When we come into coherence with others, we become catalysts for transformation, creating a ripple effect of aligned energy that expands far beyond us.

Consider a person swinging on a swing. When another person comes along and pushes them in the same direction, more force is created and the swing will go faster and higher. Now let's imagine that you want to grow in your profession with the purpose of doing more good for society and that you're coherent in your intentions and motivations. When you meet co-workers who also want to grow and have the same purpose, the resonance created will cause them and the company itself to grow. If someone's desire to grow is based simply on greed, with a goal of earning more money than others, that destructive motivation will bring dissonance to the group. Ultimately, this will prevent the company and employees from achieving their dreams and destroy the organization. (This is the reason our society and economies need reframing too.)

We can amplify energy with the same frequency and destroy it with a different one. Even if two individuals or organizations are on the same frequency and have the exact same intention, if their motivations don't merge, the outcome will fall short of what they'd hoped for, maybe drastically so. This is why my first objective in working with most clients is to help them become individually coherent and collectively shift from dissonance to resonance. I explained to the Clay brothers that as family members, they were resonant with each other because their intentions and motivations were constructive within the context of their established relationships, but when they interacted about the company, they entered into dissonance. Although what they wanted was the same—harmony in the family and prosperity—they were motivated by fear of discussing subjects that might lead to irreconcilable differences and ultimately lead to the breakup of the company. They were in avoidance mode, and this led them to make negative assumptions about each other. Nobody really knew what the others truly wanted; they just went along with the solutions that they thought would preserve the peace. Some of the brothers were focused on the past, wanting to re-create the family dynamics that existed when their father was alive. It was hard for them to plan for the future without first "fixing" the present. Others wanted to focus exclusively on the future, on growing the business to ensure ongoing prosperity for later generations of their family—no looking back. I agreed that both the past and the future were important to consider, but more important was to align on how they saw the past and what they wanted for the future.

"The past should be a learning experience, and the future should be a common goal," I said. "When your intentions are aligned, your individual concerns can complement each other, and the power of collective intention will be unleashed. And collective intention is much stronger than the sum of your individual ones."

Imagine you're pursuing your dream at work, but your motivation is rooted in the fear of being fired—a destructive driver. As a result, you'll probably find yourself out of sync with those who are also following their dreams but are motivated by the desire to create value for the company and contribute to society—a constructive motivation. Even if you love what you do and excel at it, operating from fear creates incoherence—you're clear about your intentions but unaware of the destructive motivations driving you away from them and usually toward what you want to avoid. You might tell yourself you love your work and yet you avoid taking any bold or innovative steps for fear of losing your job. This misalignment blocks you from making the kinds of decisions that lead to the best results.

This is what was happening with the Clay family, and to help them move out of dissonance, I shared the power of reframing with them.

When we see that somebody is in a negative mode—for example, one of the brothers was opposed to bringing his children into the business because of the potential for infighting with their uncles—and we know they have the same intention as we have, we can bring them into a positive mode by reframing their motivation. And when we're facing a collective challenge, we want to be motivated by our desire to find the best solutions, not by fear or anger or avoidance. When fear and anger prevail, the solutions we find might actually work against the outcome we want. When our collective motivation is constructive, we have a much better chance of achieving our vision.

I advised the brothers to identify the times when they started dissonating with each other and to counteract it by aligning their minds and hearts and their intentions and motivations and resonating instead. "This way you can bring your focus back to what you want and what you love instead of what you fear," I said. "Your actions can be based on love and finding the right way forward by seeking collaboration, identifying a higher purpose, doing whatever is needed toward your dream to build a positive legacy together."

I also explained that not only did they have the power to shift themselves from dissonance to resonance, but that they could also help to shift others. When I was young, my mother said, "If you want peace, say yes to peace. Saying no to war is putting more energy into it." Saying no to war fuels negative motivation because the intention is not constructive and, in turn, diminishes coherence, while saying yes to peace fuels positive motivation with a constructive intention and enhances coherence. Saying no to war may end in dissonance because peace won't necessarily be the result of fighting war. But those who work in favor of peace will find all the solutions they need to reach their objective. Although both groups have the same intentions, what drives them is different, and what they'll inspire in other people is also different. Saying no to war will negatively affect the larger community by fueling the energy of war, while saying yes to peace creates an energy and frequency in the community that supports its success, fueling the energy of peace.

The same applies at work, at home, and anywhere else. "Imagine you're coherent," I told the brothers, "with your heart and mind in perfect alignment. You love your job and have a clear vision of what you want to do. It's still possible for your coherence to be affected by your environment or the people around you, but if you notice that others are in dissonance, you have a chance to shift them by increasing your own internal coherence. For example, if you have a strong purpose, you can share why you love your job and how it makes a difference for you. Expressing your thoughts and strong beliefs can make all the difference."

When we pay close attention to what's happening with others—how they think, what they value, what's truly driving their behavior—we gain the insight needed to foster resonance instead of dissonance. By tuning in to the motivations that shape the environment around us, we can consciously act in ways that bring alignment. And when we act with intention and constructive motivation, we begin to influence the system—not by force, but through coherence. Our presence becomes a ripple that helps others find clarity on how to align their purpose with their motivations in their own actions.

When we understand how to shift from dissonance to resonance, we can help others be more coherent and achieve their individual dreams while also benefiting the collective well-being. Ultimately, an environment where everyone can thrive and prosper will be created.

Resonance Activates and Amplifies

The family members I was mentoring were aware of the negative effect they could have on each other, and they knew that the negativity was contagious, but they weren't as aware of the *positive* effect they could have on each other. We can spread love and joy just like we can spread fear and anger. When we're vulnerable and express our intention and motivation, we can evoke the same "energy" in others and enter into resonance with them. This resonance creates a ripple effect that can have an impact beyond the people directly involved, showing them how to live in this higher energy by consciously expressing their intentions and motivations.

One of the brothers asked me to share an example, and I told them about an experience I had when I was working in the Latin America regional office of Bayer Pharma, in Mexico City. We'd start every morning by meeting at the corner coffee stand near our office, and I noticed how we could set the tone for the whole day during those fifteen minutes of socializing. If it was raining, I might say something like, "I don't like waking up to this rain. I'm tired of getting soaked walking across the parking lot. Why does the rainy season have to last so long?" Everyone would agree that the rain was a pain and give their own reason why they didn't like it. Then we'd complain a little more as a group, eventually expanding our complaints to other things we didn't like, before heading inside and reporting to our respective offices. Eventually, I noticed that on the days that we started with an unproductive mood, motivated by destructive emotions, we weren't especially collaborative and our meetings didn't go so great.

Then I decided to conduct an experiment. Now when we'd meet for coffee, I'd say something like, "On my way here I noticed how beautiful and green all the gardens and the parks are, thanks to all this rain. Have you noticed that?" Everyone would comment on positive changes they'd seen—"Yes! My garden is very beautiful and the trees are blossoming," "I noticed that the air is much less polluted"—and speak appreciatively of the rainy season. Ultimately, we'd bring the conversation around to other things we appreciated, and these days' meetings would flow better and our collaboration would improve.

We can bring others to resonance by living our truth and expressing ourselves. Whatever we say and do affects others, so our responsibility for our actions is much bigger than we might think. When I asked the members of the Clay family how they wanted to affect each other, they all expressed a sincere desire to have a positive impact. So to help them unleash their collective potential, I explained how they could align their individual intentions and motivations with an intention and motivation they all shared. "This will create resonance," I said, "and that will enable you to accomplish bigger and better things together."

Coherence Unleashes Exponential Potential

In quantum physics, *coherence* refers to a physical system's ability to **remain stable even when influenced by outside forces; it maintains its original nature and doesn't fall apart under pressure.** In my WorkCoherence model for leading a more prosperous life, coherence is the ability to keep ourselves in a constant state regardless of our interactions with people, situations and circumstances. When we're completely coherent, our core is so strong that no external influence can emotionally affect us. Our minds (thoughts and intentions) and our hearts (emotions and motivations) are aligned, our selves unified rather than divided by conflicting agendas. We're able to leverage others' intentions and keep learning and evolving. If each person in a relationship, family, group or team learns to live in this state of coherence, collective resonance becomes exponentially easier to achieve. For the Clay family, supporting each other would create a resonance that would leverage their desire to leave a positive legacy. They realized that if they continued to dissonate and remain incoherent with each other, it could cost them not only their businesses but also their family's harmony.

For many years, I believed that being strong meant getting back at people who aren't good to us. There are times in life when revenge is socially justified because you've been hit hard by circumstances. But I've since realized that being strong really means being coherent with my belief that we should be intrinsically kind and good. If I believe in those values, I need to maintain my kindness even when society wouldn't hold me to that standard. Even when my emotions tell me I should display strength by fighting back against a bully—and even when I know that those in my environment will judge me for being fragile or weak—my coherence leads me to treat the bully with kindness. Sticking to your values and beliefs no matter what happens is true strength. And it demonstrates how *you* would like to be treated. It won't always work out that way, but when others do behave the way you'd like, a coherence will be created that will benefit all of us.

The Master has no mind of her own.
She works with the mind of the people.
She is good to people who are good.
She is also good to people who aren't good.
This is true goodness.
She trusts people who are trustworthy.
She also trusts people who aren't trustworthy.
This is true trust.
The Master's mind is like space.
People don't understand her.
They look to her and wait.
She treats them like her own children.
Tao Te Ching, verse 49, by Lao Tzu, translated by Stephen Mitchell

Living with coherence means that when we're with our families, friends, colleagues, bosses, or anyone else, we're the same person we are when we're alone. It means that no matter what's happening or when it's happening, we know who we are and act accordingly. It also means we're always open to learning experiences that support our purpose and are flexible enough to broaden our perspective when our beliefs and values are challenged.

Coherence isn't just a matter of values and choices—it's also deeply biological. As I shared with the Clay brothers, our emotions aren't just feelings. They act like a chain reaction, starting in the brain and rippling outward. When we experience an emotion, the brain fires specific patterns of electrical activity called brainwaves, measured in frequencies (cycles per second, or Hertz). Each type of wave reflects a different state of mind and body. Delta waves (0.5 cycles per second/4 Hertz) dominate in deep sleep, when the body restores and heals. Theta waves (4–7 Hz) appear in moments of meditation, daydreaming, or deep creativity. Alpha waves (8-12 Hz) emerge when we're relaxed yet alert, often linked to calm focus and positive emotions. Beta waves (13-30 Hz) rise during concentration, problem-solving, or stress, and they can become strong enough to bring anxiety. At the highest speeds, gamma waves (30-80 Hz) are associated with insight, learning, and moments of integration when the brain pulls information together into a bigger picture.

But the impact of emotions doesn't stop at the brain. These brainwave patterns influence the nervous system, which acts as the body's communication network. The nervous system carries electrical signals throughout, affecting everything from our heart rate and breathing to muscle tension and hormone production. In essence, our emotions set the brainwaves in motion, creating a cascade of electrical activity that modulates our entire body's **frequency and energy levels.** And this energetic signature isn't confined to us. We unconsciously communicate this energy to those around us. So the brothers' shared emotions were shaping not only their conversations but also their collective frequency. Their biology.

To understand how different emotional frequencies create new patterns when they're put together, consider the colors in a painting. Each color has a different frequency, and when two colors are mixed, one might dominate but a new color will emerge with a new frequency. An emotion creates a unique energy frequency in our body, and when your thoughts shift or a new situation emerges, your frequency will change. The same thing happens between two or more people. Every human interaction brings a new frequency and a new emotion. Whether it happens at home, at work, or in society, an exchange of frequencies generates new emotions and possibilities.

Now imagine if we could become aware of the frequency we're emitting through our emotions and of the collective frequency of every space we enter, be it a family dinner, a board meeting, or a global conference. With that awareness, we could intentionally choose our thoughts, words, and behaviors in ways that elevate the energy of those around us. We could design environments that naturally support trust, collaboration, and growth.

Well, guess what—it's all possible, and many of us are already doing it without realizing it. The key is becoming conscious of it so we can lead with coherence and use this power to shape healthier systems, stronger organizations, and a more fulfilling life. When individuals and organizations interact, they can enter into harmony or not depending on their individual frequencies (motivations + intentions). Every interaction we have influences the larger systems we belong to, and when we carry a destructive emotion from one system—like stress from work—it inevitably spreads into another, such as our families at the end of the day. The opposite is also true: When we nurture coherence in one part of our lives, that constructive frequency strengthens our ability to uplift every other system we touch. If we're aware of this and start to live a more intentional life, we can consciously choose which frequencies we transmit.

Every emotion carries a frequency that shapes our brain, our body, and our impact. Fear and anger pull us into incoherence, acceptance brings balance, and love, compassion, and gratitude elevate us into our highest states of coherence. And this is the beauty of being human: Our internal frequency becomes the energy that moves through spaces, relationships, and systems, multiplying what we choose to cultivate within. Coherence multiplies just like destructive energy does, and when we live in that state, we create ripples of trust, clarity, and harmony across all the systems we're part of.

TABLE 1

Emotional States, Brainwave Patterns, and Physiological Coherence

Level of Consciousness	Predominant Emotional States	Dominant Brainwave Patterns*	Autonomic Nervous System Tendency	Breathing Pattern	Heart Rhythm & HRV	Coherence State
Low Consciousness	Fear, anger, shame, chronic stress	Predominant **high beta** (≈18–30 Hz); fragmented activity	Sympathetic dominance (fight–flight)	Rapid, shallow, irregular	Erratic heart rhythm; **low HRV**	Incoherence
Emerging / Transitional Consciousness	Acceptance, openness, emotional regulation	Predominant **alpha** (≈8–12 Hz); reduced beta	Mixed autonomic balance	Slower, more rhythmic	Stabilizing rhythm; **moderate HRV**	Emerging coherence
High Consciousness	Love, compassion, gratitude	**Theta–gamma coupling** (≈4–7 Hz + 30–80 Hz); integrated networks	Parasympathetic dominance	Slow, deep, coherent	Efficient, coherent heart rhythm; **high HRV**	Peak coherence

Our World Is Built with Systems

We try to solve education problems in the education sector, we try to solve family problems at the family level, our children's school problems at school, a work problem at work. How many times have our bosses told us to leave our family problems at home? But this kind of fragmented thinking reflects an old, siloed worldview. The world operates through interconnected systems. Our lives don't happen in compartments. We don't stop being parents when we enter a boardroom, and we don't stop being professionals when we sit down for dinner with our children. The systems we're part of—family, work, education, society—aren't isolated; they're interdependent and, unlike mechanical systems, behave more like complex adaptive systems (CAS), networks of interactions that adapt to internal and external changes. And we as individuals are the bridge that connects all those systems.

The idea is that any living system can adapt when facing any challenge, not alone but with whatever created the challenge. A CAS doesn't evolve in isolation. Everything adapts through interaction. In nature, a forest that experiences prolonged storms will change the way its species live and grow, and over time those species will influence the climate and the land in return. The system responds and reshapes itself. Or consider the relationship between the human body and its gut microbiome. What once may have been seen as a harmful intruder becomes, through mutual adaptation, a symbiotic ally, offering emotional and physical benefits as the body learns to cooperate rather than defend.

Just as nature adapts, organizations and individuals that embrace complexity can evolve with resilience and creativity. Airbnb, for instance, grew as a decentralized system that adapts to local demands, mirroring the fluidity of natural ecosystems. Similarly, W.L. Gore & Associates (known for Gore-Tex) has been thriving through a self-managed, non-hierarchical structure that fosters innovation since 1967. These companies don't resist complexity—they move with it. They're alive systems, and they thrive by cultivating coherence across their interconnected parts. Leaders and businesses that adopt this mindset find new solutions by embracing the complexity of the systems they operate in instead of fighting against it.

We're all part of several systems that can influence us and that we have the power to influence. Becoming aware of how the environments we inhabit are constantly shaping our biology, emotions, and even our future selves can be a powerful exercise in intentionality. Neuroscience shows us that our surroundings leave biological imprints—on our stress levels, our mindset, our genes—but the influence isn't one-directional. Just as environments shape us, we shape them through the emotions, language, and behaviors we bring into each space. By being conscious of this double effect, we can choose to both protect ourselves from destructive influences and actively cultivate coherence in our environments, creating a ripple of constructive impact that benefits everyone connected to the system. When we understand that coherence and resonance are not uniformity but dynamic alignment within diversity, we stop trying to control everything and start co-evolving with the systems we're part of. Being aware of how our own motivations—constructive or destructive—affect not only our decisions but also the emotional and relational ecosystems around us is essential. This is the shift that allows business to flourish and life to feel meaningful.

To my delight, the Clay brothers came to this realization. They understood that their individual and collective challenges weren't something to suppress or escape from but to live fully and grow through. They transformed the impact of their environment from destructive to constructive by changing how they behaved and communicated. In the case of the brother who initially opposed bringing his children into the business, his motivation shifted from the avoidance of fights among nieces, nephews and uncles to a desire to see the company thrive under the direction of the next generation—a generation strongly motivated by their responsibility to live and leave a family legacy of good communication and openness. And a brother who'd been suffering from repeated conflicts with another stopped resisting and began embodying the love he longed to feel in the relationship. He moved from fear and frustration to compassion and clarity, from reacting to creating. And in doing so, he stepped into the legacy their father had envisioned—not just through words or plans but through the way he chose to live, lead, and love his siblings. In the end, all the brothers found harmony by aligning their individual purposes and motivations with their shared purpose to honor and further their father's legacy. This brought them into resonance and freed their collective potential, and they were now equipped to spread the goodness far and wide.

Coherent leaders see the emerging future and welcome it with adaptability, flexibility, and a clear purpose for themselves and their organizations. They share their purpose and vision for the future with their teams and employees, and with each new challenge that new world dynamic presents, they evolve their purpose and vision. They use their organization and technology to develop products and services that offer solutions to problems created with a lack of consciousness, including environmental destruction. And they understand that by shaping environments with constructive decisions, they can create ripple effects that influence all the other systems their organization touches.

Whether the Clay family rises to the challenges ahead and makes the impact they hope for depends only on how much they want to continue learning, to strengthen their hearts and souls, to live a coherent life, and to foster their resonance by always focusing on the beautiful legacy they want to leave. They have the tools and the heart to do so, and the world would thank them for it.

Whatever the case, I was grateful for the opportunity to work with some members of the next generation and pass on some of what I've learned, and I was thrilled to see them embrace it so fully. It reinforced my hope that that generation and those to follow will shape the future with strong hearts and wise minds.

CHAPTER 2

WE LIVE IN A QUANTUM SYSTEM

Systems are made up of all the elements working together in mechanisms, networks, principles, and procedures, and yet we tend to study each element in isolation. My mother used to point to the separation of medicine and psychology as the perfect example of what's wrong with not looking at the big picture. She said that in trying to cure disease by looking at the body as a purely mechanical entity, we miss important clues to what caused or aggravated the disease. The circumstances that one person lived in and their emotional state could have been contributing factors; the disease itself may have only been a manifestation of something that was wrong with the big picture.

In the *Oxford English Dictionary*, the definitions of *system* are:

- a set of things working together as parts of a mechanism or an interconnecting network
- the state railroad system
- a set of principles or procedures according to which something is done, an organized framework or method
- the public school system

Today we know the importance of mental health and its effects on our bodies. Most MDs don't just look at a disease in isolation; they also look at a patient's medical and life history so they can see the whole picture. And this is the approach we should take to *everything*, observing and analyzing our lives as part of a bigger context so we can make solid, well-informed decisions.

So just what *is* the big picture? How much of what's around us do we need to consider in order to make good decisions?

In 2002, I was business manager for Bayer in Europe, responsible for Greece, the Netherlands and Belgium. After starting with the company in 1996 in Brazil, I was thrilled to have the opportunity of an expatriate career in my early thirties. It was to be a three- to five-year gig in a position traditionally filled by young people being groomed to take over as heads of other countries' operations. I was happy to learn the dynamics of the headquarters in Leverkusen, Germany, and did my best to learn German, but after just a year and a half, my boss called me into his office and told me the Hungarian general manager was stepping down, and he wanted me to take over *that* position.

I couldn't even picture Hungary on the map in my mind, and a colleague had recently happened to mention that Hungarian was an even more complex language to learn than German. It might as well have been another universe. On top of that, I'd face enormous management challenges, given that the country was about to join the Eurozone.

It would be an intimidating transition, but I'd always made it clear that I was eager to go wherever I could be of the most service, and if my boss believed I was the best fit for the job, I should be happy to accept it. Even if I had doubts that I was the right person, it was an opportunity to learn and serve. I had to trust my boss. I knew that if I worked with the circumstances that had created this new challenge instead of resisting it, I'd be able to rise to the occasion and beyond. So, excited to broaden my horizons *again*, I started Hungarian lessons.

If I'd made my decision based only on what I could see and feel, I'd have lost an opportunity that my boss could see *for* me. The fact that an idea seems to come from outside our systems doesn't mean it's not the perfect course of action for us. Its appearance in our lives is a *product* of our own systems (in my case, a system emerged as a consequence of my intention to serve where I would be most useful). When we can see the big picture, we can see systems that are part of worlds we don't belong to at that moment in time, worlds that *others* can connect our potential to.

In my case, what others saw that I only later came to see was a part of me that excelled in dealing with complexity and leading through challenges, uniting diversities and polarities toward a common vision. A part of me that, in hindsight, I could see had been awakened by looking for management and leadership lessons differently from the way most executives go about it. My mother obviously saw it. After I accepted the position in Hungary, she sent me books about business and selections from her own readings that she thought would be helpful; books that created intersections between science, spirituality, and ancient philosophies. Among them were the biography of German physicist Werner Heisenberg; *The Tao of Physics* by Fritjof Capra; and *Spiritual Quotient* by Professor Danah Zohar. These books brought me language for speaking about spirituality within organizations, part of the leadership style I was building for myself.

Meanwhile, I'd also started studying Yoga philosophy by way of the *Yoga Sutras* and Ashtanga yoga classes. And Bayer hired an executive coach, Penny Sophocleous, who brought a more human perspective on leadership than I would have gotten by taking courses and workshops and reading articles in the *Harvard Business Review.*

Through all these explorations, I was getting to know myself and my behavior better and coming to understand the spirituality of communities and countries and their behavior within various situations and circumstances. It was a journey of both self-discovery and discovery of the systems around me. And what I found was that the more I broadened my searches, the easier it became for me to think of solutions that would make the complex simple. And none of it would have happened if I'd "trusted" my fears. Instead, I trusted my mother's guidance and aimed to be the best possible version of myself, and in the process, I realized my potential in a way that wouldn't have been possible if I hadn't come to understand the systems around me.

We Are the Most Important System

"The privilege of a lifetime is to become who you truly are."
– Carl Jung

As human beings, we pursue the survival of ourselves and the systems we live in. Those systems include families, communities, schools, organizations, governments and even fauna and flora in nature, and they all work together. But how do we learn to stop viewing them as isolated as we try to solve problems and build our plans for the future?

In the late 2000s, the complexity of our world started to force us all to change how we looked for solutions to problems. Globalization, rapid technological advancements, and interconnectedness across various domains created an intricate web of cause-and-effect relationships. Clearly, we could no longer solve a problem by isolating it. New challenges that countries and individuals faced were all connected. Emerging pandemics and the exploitation of human resources without regard for the consequences were intertwined problems, and suddenly we were in need of much better human coordination across the planet.

In 2008, a new concept gained popularity among executives at big corporations and in government and was embraced by leaders around the world as complex challenges emerged. The concept was *systems thinking*—the ability to take a helicopter view and see a problem as a series of connected dots instead of a collection of isolated dots. The world was starting to understand the importance of coherence among systems and the elements that are part of it.

Distinctions between professional and personal life and between organization and employee faded as we started to see that there's no separation between them. Instead of solving problems by sacrificing the interests of one or the other, we realized that the interests of both need to be taken into consideration. For decades, the business world has demanded that people leave their problems at home and be emotionally balanced at work. Therapies were even developed to help employees achieve this "balance." Easy enough for a robot, right? Likewise, we tend to feel pressure to leave work problems at the office and arrive home smiling for the sake of our families. The solution to the quest for balance is to regard our work self and our home self as the same self who's just moving back and forth between places. When we can do that, everything gets much easier. Separating who we are in our different systems only distances us from who we really are.

When I decided to accept a certain position because it made sense for me given what else was happening in my life, my family accepted the jobs with me. The decision wasn't just mine—we had a family meeting, and if a job would allow us to live our purpose, everyone would be onboard. My family was part of my work, living its challenges and triumphs with me and giving me their full support. And at the office, my colleagues knew how important this work was to my family, and when I had a challenge at home I could count on my organization to have my back. My family would understand when I needed to work extra hours, and my colleagues would understand when I needed to give my attention to an important event involving my husband or children. The key was not to isolate my family from my work but to make the necessary connections between them by being vulnerable, open, honest—*myself*—in all my manifestations: mother, wife, sister, daughter and head of a company.

Changing the way I saw balance in my life changed how the balance was reached, and as a result, my well-being has improved tremendously. Acknowledging the systems I live in and making the connections among them was truly a life-changer.

We're All Connected—It's Not Just a Saying

"When we strive to become better than we are,
everything around us becomes better too."
—Paulo Coelho

By understanding the basic concepts of coherence, resonance, and dissonance, we can see how much we're affected by the relationships we have and the environment we live in. If we aren't aware of this, we'll wake up one day filled with regret, seeing how relationships and environments have negatively influenced us, with no hope of saving ourselves. This is why midlife crises happen to so many people. It's simple cause and effect. If we are aware that working with complex adaptive systems changes how we see and approach things, we start to notice that everything we do somehow affects everything else. When all the connections are made, things fall into place because we're acknowledging their interaction. In quantum physics, this is called "entanglement." Everything that's connected can't be described as separate from each other—they're entangled.

Wikipedia describes it like this:

> *Quantum entanglement is a quantum mechanical phenomenon in which the quantum states of two or more objects have to be described with reference to each other, even though the individual objects may be spatially separated … For example, it is possible to prepare two particles in a single quantum state such that when one is observed to be spin-up, the other one will always be observed to be spin-down and vice versa … As a result, measurements performed on one system seem to be instantaneously influencing other systems entangled with it.*

So we can't describe one object as being isolated from another. They exist in relation to each other. At the moment of birth, we become entangled with everything around us—our families, our communities, our governments, our countries. And throughout our lives, the decisions we make affect all our systems and the effects can occur on the other side of the world.

When we're part of a system, we interfere with it, and if we aren't conscious of this, we might cause unintended consequences within the system. For example, in the era of Nazism, Hitler used the power of aligning negative intentions and motivations to influence millions of Germans and other nations with Nazi propaganda that would become their north star until they woke up too late to the consequences of their acts. Ultimately, they would pass on regrets to generations to come. Many who have helped perpetrate massacres have reported initially believing they were doing something good for humanity, obviously influenced by the environment, language, and behaviors they were immersed in.

In recent decades, the widespread access to information has greatly changed the way that the power to manipulate the masses is used. With very clear ideas about how to live their lives, the younger generations have brought about a beautiful shift in the way agendas are fulfilled. The Arab Spring was an example of an event fueled by the use of social media to realize the wishes of a group of people who were demanding freedom, dignity, and human rights. Protests of government corruption and resulting economic crises started in Tunisia and spread across the Arab world thanks to the power of social media. But this wasn't an isolated event. Just months later, the Occupy Movement began in New York City's Zuccotti Park with the slogan "We are the 99%," protesting economic inequality, corporate influence, and political corruption. At the same time, thousands of Spanish youths peacefully protested austerity and unemployment and demanded the creation of decentralized assemblies and direct democratic practices. And in Chile and the United Kingdom, mass mobilizations of students demanding free education and fair policies took place almost in synchrony. These events shared emotional energy: frustration, awakening, and a will to co-create new systems. Social media, economic hardship, and youth values acted as resonant forces, producing similar waves in different geographies. This is the entanglement of systems.

In our day-to-day lives, this entanglement can be observed in the systemic thinking that companies now employ in looking at their performance. In the past, it was common for one individual to be seen as a star and given a big bonus, or for a CEO to be the most important figure in an organization, but today it's clear that the power of the collective is much more important than individual stars. And there's a growing awareness of the impact that overuse of resources has on our future, with corporations coming to understand that the impact they have in society and the world is much more important than simply creating a need for their products and services and selling them.

When we understand that we live in a systemic world, it's clear that we influence what's around us at the same time as we're *being* influenced. Every thought we have and every action we decide to take, consciously or unconsciously, is a result of the impact of the people around us and the world we live in—and, in turn, every action we take will influence those same people and that same world.

The way our world has affected us—in other words, our past and the way we *perceive* our past, the stories we tell ourselves about people and situations— affect everything we think and do in the present and shape our future. And this can benefit us as much as it can interfere with our well-being. Albert Einstein said, "The most important decision we make is whether we believe we live in a hostile or friendly universe," and if we think we live in a hostile universe, the decisions we make will be targeted to avoidance and self-defense. On the other hand, if we believe we live in a friendly universe, we'll aim for abundance; we'll recognize that the possibilities are limitless and make decisions accordingly. And these decisions will impact our relationships and our environment, with new dynamics emerging and transformations occurring.

Imagine that a person has decided he doesn't want to continue at his workplace because of dissonance—lack of resonance—with his supervisor and the environment but has to be there for a couple of months more. If he isn't conscious of his influence on the workplace, his attitude might lead the other members of his team to shift their own attitudes in the same negative direction. And if it turns out that, at the end of the two months, he's offered his boss's position and decides to stay, the negative impact he had on the team may ultimately result in difficulties in leading those people. But if he decides to start creating a positive legacy by enjoying those two months and inspiring his coworkers to work for the sake of their own honor and their purpose, by the time he's offered his boss's position, he'll have nurtured the soil where he needs to plant his seeds. And chances are those plants will flourish, whether he stays or leaves. And he'll have adopted the right mindset for whatever he does next.

The stories we tell ourselves dictate our future. Whether they're positive or negative, they're what our future will look like. If we're conscious of how our actions influence others and how those actions can come back to haunt or bless us, we'll be more likely to act in ways that allow us to build the futures we want.

We Can Use the Power of Connected Systems to Create the Future

By using connected coherent systems, we can create a new level of complexity that benefits everyone on the planet. Consider the "Greta Thunberg effect." Greta is a global activist from Sweden who in 2020 became the youngest female to open the World Economic Forum's annual meeting in Davos, Switzerland, at age seventeen. She started her campaign in 2018 by protesting in front of the Swedish parliament, holding a sign that read *School strike for climate.* Since then, she's gone on to become the symbol of activism for climate change, and the strength and belief with which she's lived has influenced millions of people of all ages and beliefs around the world.

When she opened the Davos meeting, it was the start of a global shift toward reverting the negative impact our lifestyles are having on climate and the planet in general. In February 2019, Jean-Claude Juncker, president of the European Commission, announced plans to allocate a quarter of the EU's budget to climate change mitigation in February 2019. And in January 2021, the *Journal of Applied Social Psychology* published research that found increased consciousness of climate change as a result of Greta's protests, along with a greater sense of collective efficacy—the belief that through working together with like-minded others, we can reduce global warming—and a greater commitment to taking collective action.

It's quantum coherence and entanglement in action. Greta achieved coherence by maintaining her beliefs and transmitting her message in environments with the potential to influence and intimidate her. With her strong and clear purpose and her knowledge of who she is and her role in her own life, she was able to remain a force of nature and positively influence those who knew of her quest. She had the power to impact systems that were entangled with her, no matter how the entanglement happened.

Once we understand how entanglement among systems works, we can work to bring systems together to unleash their potential and achieve our intentions faster. When Greta voiced her beliefs at age fifteen, she inspired millions, and within two years she was able to take her case to real change-makers. She used her strong belief and sense of purpose to navigate through systems. Rather than being weakened by them, as usually happens when people are intimidated by authorities, she used them to reinforce her purpose. When we align our intentions, enter into coherence and resonate with others, the systems' power is unleashed.

To be coherent as an individual is to have the ability to align our intentions with the right motivations and maintain this alignment even in the face of external interferences, challenges, or unplanned events. When that happens, our purpose allows us to adapt and change according to circumstances and keep our intentions and motivations aligned toward our purpose—our true north. And when that happens, external interference will always be constructive interference, be it a positive or negative experience, pushing us to learn and bringing us closer to our purpose. When we integrate external interference into our journey, we speed our learning curve, and that allows us to help others do the same. Interference is destructive only if it interrupts our coherence and our journey to purpose.

Take the human body as an example of coherence. If the body is in coherence, or balance, all its systems—digestive, circulatory, immunologic, reproductive—will work with each other to fulfill the purpose of keeping the person alive and well. Any external interference such as bacteria will create a temporary need for a new balance, which will require one system or another to work harder than usual. When the overall system is in harmony, it's easier to detect any negative interference and create a defense, and the interference will ultimately prove to be constructive because it helped build resilience; the body either strengthens its immune system by fighting the bacteria or simply learns to live with it. And these learned responses can be repeated if the interference recurs at some point. But if the system is unbalanced and tired, any external interference can be destructive, working against its purpose of keeping the body alive. So it's critical that we keep bringing our body back into coherence.

For a society to be coherent, individuals need to align their individual purposes with a common intention that benefits both the collective and the individual. A collective that resonates is stronger, and a collective awareness of the existing interferences is crucial to maintaining this resonance. It's also important to be aware of the motivations behind the collective system's decisions. If the system starts to make decisions based on destructive emotions raised by external interferences, there will be a loss of alignment and coherence, and the system will dissonate and destroy itself. On the flip side, learning how to act when external interferences require us to make changes in order to remain aligned with our purpose will make the system stronger. If a new player or a newly elected public official interferes with our harmony, for example, we can learn from the experience and strengthen our resolve. Being aware of the interference occurring in all the systems around us is key to leveraging its power to enhance our coherence.

If we want more equality, justice, and harmony as a society, we need to be able to express ourselves and reinforce our intentions, which requires knowing our motivations. And we need to realize that motivations will change. We need to be prepared when they become destructive—that way, we'll be able to help each other bring our intentions and motivations back into alignment.

Many success stories that later turn to failure have something in common: They didn't consider other systems, meaning they couldn't maintain their coherence with their purpose and entered into dissonance with the interference around them. They subscribed to the belief that you don't argue with a winning formula. But what brought you success this time might work against you next time, and we need to adapt to the new dynamics that will always be emerging. The only constant in life is change, and being in synchronicity with change will give you leverage to learn what's necessary to building the future. Learning and evolution shouldn't be regarded as optional. We should welcome those around us who challenge our status quo; we need them to keep us on our toes.

Kodak found this out the hard way. With a clear intention and purpose—to preserve memories on film and paper—the company had become the market leader. Its people were passionate about the company's purpose, and this fed their success over the years. But when digital technology appeared on the scene, Kodak dropped the ball. The top executives still believed in their purpose, but they were motivated more by fear—fear of the financial loss that might result from taking a risk. The result was their exit from the market. Kodak's leadership clearly wasn't aware of our uncontrollable entanglement with technology and the speed of information. No company has the power to stop progress. Although they can slow it down for a while, the consequences will always come in the form of a high price to pay.

While the systems that make up our world can't be controlled, one thing *is* under our control: We have the power to build on each other's intentions and motivations to resonate. And clarity about each other's purpose is key to finding a common intention and resonating further. If each one of us can put into words our own intentions and be aware of the motivation behind our actions, we'll all be much more conscious and our opportunities to resonate will expand exponentially.

There's Immense Power in Coherence and Resonance

Because Greta Thunberg was clear about her intentions and motivations and leveraged the systems around her to spread her message, it resonated with many others who took on her purpose as their own. And living this kind of coherent life has applications beyond building our own future. Leveraging the systems around us also allows us to improve our world for the next generations and inspire those generations to do the same. And *this* can result in collective efficacy on a greater and greater scale.

Like humans, countries and businesses have life spans, evolving as a result of their interactions with each other. When they learn to see the big system and channel their potential into working together in harmony, they can help bring prosperity to the world. When countries' intentions and motivations align, they help humanity make sustainable progress. The United Nations' Sustainable Development Goals (SDG) are a perfect example of countries working together to tackle common challenges whose resolutions will have long-term benefits for us all. By speaking a common language, they were able to create the seventeen goals that people from all parts of the world, of different origins and cultures, can pursue jointly—goals aimed at benefiting the planet and all of humanity.

As for businesses, no one will win if the goal is to steal the market from the other players rather than to benefit all people and the planet. There's an abundance of need on Earth, and if businesses shared the intention to focus on the greatest possible good and cooperated with each other toward that end, many of the biggest problems we face could be solved. Governments would be able to focus on the governance needed to progress further instead of enforcing rules and regulations to prevent people and businesses from destroying themselves.

Coherence in Life

"Try to accept the changing seasons of your heart, even if you have seen them before. With each change, life is remade, and so are you."
—Rumi

To live a coherent life, we have to be open to all the lessons life provides us. Deciding to be a lifelong learner is the best way to become more coherent. Lifelong learners learn about and from the systems they're part of in each step of their life's journey. Seeing all the systems we belong to and living a holistic life, not centered on what immediately surrounds us, can significantly enhance our wisdom. This also implies being aware of the stories you're telling yourself about your past and about what you want from your future. Going forward, your learning will allow you to build stories of your choosing, and your intentional choices will align your mind (thoughts and intentions) and your heart (emotions and motivations). This is a movement from intelligence to wisdom, bringing you awareness of both the intentional and the unintentional, or passive, decisions you're making in life.

Once we learn to be open to the wisdom all around us and we recognize the systems that make up our world, we can also see how important it is to really understand our intentions and how our actions affect everything else. We start to ask questions like, "Why am I doing what I'm doing?" "Did I give myself enough time to choose correctly?" and "How will each choice affect others and my future?"

These questions can help bring coherence to our lives, but we don't want to stop there. The most important step in this journey is to bring coherence to our systems. And for this, we need to understand what makes life meaningful for us.

Work Is Life

We tend to use the term *work* to refer to what we do to earn money—our profession, our job, our business. But work is more than that. We're always working. Whenever we put effort into taking any step in our life, we're working. The question is what work we want to bring into our lives.

After we're born, our first work is to communicate the need to be fed and cleaned by others, and we do it by crying. Later, we learn that words are useful and we work on using the right words to get what we need. Eventually, we work on tending to our needs ourselves. As we mature, we work on controlling our emotions and communicating in a way that brings our hopes and desires into alignment with the expectation of others. Then our work is to figure out why we want what we want and align our expectations with those wants. The sooner we can do this, the sooner we'll be able to find internal peace.

And after all *that* work, reality hits—there's *more* work to be done. We have to leave the cocoon of home for school—we all know how hard that is—and then we have to find a profession. And then we're *still* not done. When family comes along, that means more work and more *complex* work—the work of integrating all family members and their systems into our existing work, understanding that we'll influence and be influenced by our environment *collectively*. Suddenly, we're immersed in systems that nobody taught us about. How are we supposed to bring coherence to it all? How do we know when we're resonating or dissonating with something or somebody? Why didn't they teach us the secrets of coherence in school?

Well, better late than never. Let's learn how to bring coherence to our lives *now*.

CHAPTER 3

WE CAN TRANSFORM TO BECOME CONSCIOUS HUMANS AND INSPIRING LEADERS

When Tara arrives at work, her boss is already talking to some of the team members in their cubicle. He's always early.

"When I saw the delay in your project, I was worried and a little disappointed," she hears him say. "I trusted that you'd come to talk to me if a problem came up." He shrugs. "But at least we can learn from this lesson, so it's not a total loss. How do you want to proceed?"

Tara knows how important this project is for the company, but Theodore's voice is calm. When he's upset about something, he'll let you know, but always in that calm voice. And he expects his employees to the same. At her desk, Tara remembers the day he urged them to be emotional, but with conditions.

"Do you want emotions to work for you?" he said. "Then put your feelings into words, but don't let those feelings run *faster* than your words."

Theodore isn't this way only at work. He's the same open, caring person with everybody. His kids go to the same school as Tara's kids, and she's seen how he speaks authentically with other parents, teachers, and the principal, smiling and seeming to put everyone at ease. And he's openly caring with his wife, always holding the door for her and including her in every conversation. He tells people his purpose is to make every place he goes a lighter place where others feel safe and comfortable being themselves. And it works. People visibly relax in his presence.

In working with Theodore for the past five years, Tara has learned to be vulnerable and not to react to unexpected situations. But the rules seem to be different for women. She hasn't been able to drop all her masks like Theodore has. She can be herself with her husband, but she has to be a little tough with her kids. And at work, she feels compelled to wear her badass mask because she's received feedback that she tends to be too emotional. In meetings where the others—mostly men—speak loudly and often interrupt her, she has to almost shout to be heard. She's said the phrase, "Sorry, if you'll just let me finish" so many times she hears it in her sleep.

Being a woman in a place dominated by badasses isn't easy. And when you're also a wife and a mother to four children, knowing which mask to wear at any given moment can be an emotionally exhausting challenge. Feeling like you have to be the person who meets everyone's expectations is sure to take a toll over time, and Tara is at the point where something has to give. If she's going to be truly happy, she needs to live consciously and intentionally like Theodore.

Living consciously means being aware of your impact on others and how situations and people affect you. Living intentionally means you have a reason for everything you do and don't do, and you choose the impact you want to have. Instead of immediately reacting with your emotions, you act the way you want to act even while acknowledging the emotions that have been raised.

When we're aware of our effect on others and how other people and situations affect us, we're able to live our intentions and automatically bring harmony and coherence to our families, communities, and the entire world. We can be ourselves and express our feelings and emotions in a manner that adds to others' lives instead of harming them. When we can live our deepest purpose, we align with each other almost instantly. We always know the "why" of each other and become more understanding. We come from a place of collaboration and mutual help rather than a place of selfishly searching for what's in it for us.

In the story above, Theodore brings harmony everywhere he goes. He can put into words his purpose of creating safe and comfortable spaces where people can be themselves. When dealing with different systems, he isn't changed by the energy of the systems; rather, he influences and inspires the systems to be better. The people he interacts with take his energy and his example and begin to live them. Living his purpose allows him to live exactly the life he wants and provide a model for others to follow.

Tara, on the other hand, believes she needs to adapt to each system by becoming a different person. Her focus on excelling in all her roles causes a separation between her and her world. Every time a new person, situation, or system is introduced into her life, she has to step back and consider what's expected of her and put on the appropriate mask. Inevitably, she'll lose her identity by constantly catering to expectations that might not even be accurate; it may be that she's the only one who has these expectations of herself. How can a person who's playing false versions of herself hope to inspire others? Which "Tara" are they supposed to put their faith in? What are her friends and family to think? Who *is* she?

Learning to be conscious and intentional is essential for all of us. When we learn to practice consciousness and intentionality, we make the lives of others much better, and we transform the environment around us into the place we want to live. When we don't, we lose track of who we are, and at a certain point, we'll need to ask ourselves, "What am I doing with my life? Is this person the person I want to be? Am I proud of myself?"

We were all born as "natural" human beings with the same basic needs and instincts. And we all have the ability to become *conscious* human beings who make the world a better place just because they're part of it. We all have the ability to communicate our purpose through our words and actions and inspire others, and this kind of leadership can bring about significant change in the world. People who live like Theo, achieving inner peace and equilibrium and benefiting everyone around them, create a positive future.

On the other hand, people can also "inspire" others negatively, in which case the future that's being created will bring harm to others. Some people might inspire others negatively without even realizing it. They can be financially successful and materially fulfilled, but if they haven't been true to themselves and negatively impact the world, at a certain point they'll become frustrated. They might have had the right intention, but they weren't conscious enough to remain in coherence, and they'll end up with regrets and a sense of missing something in life.

Soviet physicist Andrei Dmitrievich Sakharov was instrumental in creating the hydrogen bomb—work that brought his country superpower status—but over time he became increasingly disturbed by the destructive potential of his invention. Ultimately, his remorse led him to dedicate the latter part of his life to advocating for nuclear disarmament and human rights, a commitment that earned him the Nobel Peace Prize in 1975.

Sakharov's life illustrates how we can be drawn into actions that appear to be successful on the surface, garnering recognition and influence, but leave us feeling deeply unsettled. Many of us live our lives reacting to circumstances and situations, blindly following strict planning, and being disappointed when something goes "wrong." These are three symptoms of not living consciously and intentionally. In Tara's case, she's at the mercy of what life will bring her. She has plans for herself in the different spheres of her life, but those plans are motivated by the desire to satisfy others. When she feels unaccepted or has to conform, this brings an added level of stress.

When we aren't in coherence, it can disrupt our sense of purpose and result in harm to ourselves and others. But by embracing coherence and conscious responsibility, as Sakharov came to do, we avoid creating future harm for ourselves and others and instead design a legacy built on positive impact. If we want to participate in the designing of a positive future, we need to learn how to live a coherent, conscious life, and that begins by being proactive and responsive instead of reactive or passive. If we do this, we really *can* transform the world.

Throughout history, many highly intelligent and powerful people have dedicated themselves to teaching the power of conscious living. In *Meditations*, Roman emperor Marcus Aurelius writes about Stoicism, a lifestyle that seeks happiness through virtue. In a word, he says being good and not having attachments will make you happy. The same belief is reflected in Hinduism, Jainism, Buddhism, and other Eastern religions. People like Buddha, Rumi, and Gandhi and ancient books such as the Tao Te Ching, the Kabbalah, and the Baghavad Gita have offered guidance about living fully, teaching us to flow with life but always with the knowledge that we have the power to make a positive difference. But it isn't just people like Buddha and Gandhi who can inspire us. Our neighbors, colleagues, and mentors can inspire us to look beyond our own lives and see our place in the world and our power to impact others' lives positively—our power to transform the world.

When We're Not Conscious, We're Trapped by Our Natural Selves

"Happiness is when what you think, what you say, and what you do are in harmony."
—Mahatma Gandhi

I walk down the street.
There is a deep hole in the sidewalk.
I fall in.
I am lost… I am helpless.
It isn't my fault.
It takes forever to find a way out.
I walk down the same street.
There is a deep hole in the sidewalk.
I pretend I don't see it.
I fall in again.
I can't believe I am in the same place.
But, it isn't my fault.
It still takes me a long time to get out.
I walk down the same street.
There is a deep hole in the sidewalk.
I see it is there.
I still fall in. It's a habit.
My eyes are open.

I know where I am.
It is my fault. I get out immediately.
I walk down the same street.
There is a deep hole in the sidewalk.
I walk around it.
I walk down another street.
—*"There Is a Hole in My Sidewalk" by Portia Nelson*

As natural beings, people can live their entire lives without noticing that anything is missing. Many do. They never see the opportunity to live fully. Instead of having become conscious and intentional, they end life as they began it, as natural beings. Taking the same streets, falling into the same holes.

If you made a choice early in life but it no longer feels right, or if you achieved financial success but something still seems to be missing, those are wonderful bits of information for you to work with. Even better, they're signs that you're yearning for a more meaningful life—a conscious life.

The poem by Portia Nelson captures the regret that comes from confronting the most important decisions in life with a lack of consciousness, from choosing *not* to confront them. Even when we're aware of our mistakes, sometimes we still "can't" change how we make choices, and the consequences keep coming. The only way to break the cycle is to take responsibility—it *is* the result of our decisions. If we live life reacting to what's happening without making a change (same street, same holes), that life will be a limited one, only partially lived. But we always have the power to stop, observe what's happening, and make a different decision.

One of the characteristics of natural beings is that their perception of the world around them is limited by their spheres, or environments—family, school, friends. They overlook the importance of the community they live in, their teachers' lives, and their colleagues. Many people aren't even aware of important events in a neighboring country.

The spheres of our life grow in complexity as we get older. Depending on how we were raised, we may live selfishly and not be able to see the world around us. Most of us don't understand how critical it is to be aware of the world we live in and the connections among all the things around us. We usually don't see how simple actions and thoughts have a massive impact on our environment. And even if we *are* aware of our impact, we might not know how to act coherently in all spheres of our lives. We might act one way in our professional lives and a different way with our families and friends. Not being coherent in all parts of our lives causes us to separate the spheres of our lives, and this can have detrimental results for us. Among them, we may:

- Miss the exponential potential of using all the spheres of our lives in pursuit of what we want
- Invest an exhausting amount of energy into wearing different masks in different situations
- Never know our true selves
- Prevent others from knowing our true selves
- Fail to be reliable people

Ultimately, a lack of coherence will mean we won't be able to recognize these effects and the other ways our separated spheres work against us rather than in harmony *for* us. And if we don't understand how we got stuck in relationships and environments we didn't choose for ourselves, we also won't be able to choose our futures, no matter how "in charge" of our lives we think we are.

In early 2022, Arthur Do Val, a Brazilian congressman who was running for São Paulo governor, decided to go to Ukraine to raise awareness of the human toll of Russia's attack on the nation, earning him the praise of his vast social media following for walking his talk. After a week of fundraising and travels in the Ukraine talking to residents to find out what they needed, the Brazilian media released leaked audio messages that the rising young politician had sent to a private WhatsApp group of his soccer friends in which he described Ukrainian women waiting in refugee lines as "total goddesses" and "easy" because they were poor.

He said that he didn't have time to "engage" with any of them but that he'd go back to "enjoy" them after the war. (And these were the *least* offensive parts of his comments.)

Brazilian diplomatic officials in Ukraine made clear to the world that Do Val hadn't been on an official mission and denounced his comments. Even before he landed back in São Paulo, his party had expelled him and his girlfriend had left him. Ultimately, he had to end his candidacy for governor.

This was his statement about the matter: "These audios were mine. But they were meant to be sent only to a private group. The politician you voted for is different from the guy on the audio. The audios were for a group of male friends who wanted to tease each other. But I still apologize for them."

This is a perfect example of how people can be disconnected from their lives and what they truly want; how they can wear one mask in public and a very different one in private. And now that people can see the "whole" person thanks to social media, there's a growing demand that public figures lead coherent lives. Would Do Val have behaved the same way if he were living coherently, with a clear purpose? Or would he have doubled down on who he really was and not felt pressured by his soccer buddies to act "macho"? Would he behave like this if he knew the impact he'd have on the various relationships and environments he was part of?

Public figures and leaders need to walk their talk. They need to be the same person in all spheres of their lives. They need to dig deep inside themselves and discover who they really are, what they want, and how they want to live. Today, decisions made at a young age make a lasting impact because digital footprints last forever. You might become someone you're proud of, but choices you made in the past will always follow you. Even when we click on an online ad just out of curiosity, we create a record that others can use to define us. So we need to be conscious about even the trivial things we do. As human beings, we have the free will to think, speak, and act as we want, but we're not free of the consequences, so we need to be careful about how we use that free will.

How can a young politician or anyone else who can't walk their talk become whole and lead a coherent life? By being aware of the integrality of their lives—understanding that absolutely everything we do has either a positive or a negative impact on our lives and our surroundings—and learning to create habits by being intentional about how they live.

Being Conscious Is a Choice, and So Is Being Happy and Prosperous

"The younger you become wise, the longer you will be happy in your life."
—Oditiama Tsujisan

When I was thirteen, my grandmother died and my grandfather started coming to our house to sleep because my mother wanted to be close to him in case something happened during the night. My brother and sister and I took turns sleeping in the guest room with him, and I loved when it was my turn because we'd talk about the big issues—death, happiness, how life should be lived. One night he told me something that sounded especially important: "The younger you become wise, the longer you will be happy in your life." Those words stayed with me, but it took me a long time to understand what he meant.

Living consciously and knowing how to flow with life are part of being wise, and just like my grandfather said, the sooner you learn to be wise, the longer you'll be happier. Not because your life will become less challenging, but because you'll know how to deal with what gets in your way and keep it from growing out of proportion. You'll experience less deception, frustration, and other problems because you know where you're heading and how to deal with the obstacles along the way. The result? Happiness!

In 2015, *Forbes* reported that 20 percent of CEOs were prone to depression, twice the average rate among the rest of the population. In the article, psychologist Todd Essig pointed out that trying to find worth by looking further up the ladder is a consistently self-destructive endeavor: "Some people habitually measure their self-worth by whoever seems to be more successful than they are, a recipe for constant depression-inducing envy." The story said that as we ascend the ladder, we often lose appreciation for the simple beauties in life and depression becomes increasingly likely.

More recent studies report a rise in reported mental health struggles among CEOs, alongside a growing trend of executive departures linked to pressure and public visibility. A 2024 Businessolver report found that 55 percent of CEOs had experienced a mental health issue in the past year, a 24 percent increase over the previous year. The study also showed that 52 percent viewed their company culture as toxic and 81 percent believed that revealing mental health struggles would be seen as a sign of weakness.

Meanwhile, broader executive-level data from the *Journal of Occupational Health Psychology* shows that 26 percent of executives report symptoms consistent with clinical depression, compared with just 18 percent in the general workforce. Similarly, a 2024 *Harvard Business Review* survey reported that nearly half of CEOs feel lonely or isolated and that 61 percent believe this affects their performance.

We tend to tie our happiness to material outcomes, and while we're trying to achieve success, we might attribute a lack of happiness to the fact that we haven't achieved it yet. And then when we *have* reached a high position in the hierarchy, it turns out that accumulating wealth doesn't bring the satisfaction we expected. We're not as happy as people who have much less wealth but find meaning in their lives by serving others.

In the case of Viktor Frankl—lacking money and family and suffering atrocious abuse in a concentration camp—he found his purpose in writing his theory of logotherapy. And after leaving the camp, he became a well-known psychologist because of his passion and purpose. Despite his painful past, he built a meaningful life that gave him peace, joy, and abundance. Meanwhile, how many CEOs do we know whose lives are full of peace and joy?

In *How Will You Measure Your Life?* Harvard Business School professor Clayton M. Christensen describes how, upon retiring, many high-achieving CEOs suddenly find themselves with a deep sense of emptiness and even depression. After years spent pursuing achievements that brought them financial success and professional accolades, they realize they've neglected personal relationships and broader life purposes. Christensen uses these cautionary stories to illustrate how misguided it can be to measure success solely by career milestones and financial outcomes. Instead, he offers a framework for real fulfillment, one rooted in investing in relationships, maintaining integrity, and aligning our daily actions with a deeper sense of purpose.

The day we're born, we're thrust into a certain environment with certain people, and we go on to become a product of the interaction of the two and our interpretation of them. As we grow, spheres are added, and there's more and more for us to be aware of and care for. And as this happens, our growing consciousness will help us to be aware of what we really want to become. If we're lucky, sooner rather than later we'll shape our relationships and our environment in such a way that they'll help us create the future we want for ourselves.

Each of us has to make up our minds to live a conscious life, and this is life's beauty and magic. Every time we feel the positive consequence of this choice, the feeling grows on us, and choosing differently will make us conscious of the joyful and magic life we're giving up.

Being Conscious Requires Endurance and Resilience

You need endurance to put the lessons you're constantly learning into practice. And you need resilience to be grateful for the challenges you face despite the pain they may cause. When something unexpected happens, people who live consciously embrace the experience and come out of it with a new path or a new tool for achieving what they want. In other words, when life presents them with lemons, they make lemonade.

And to build resilience and endurance, you need one more thing: the ability to be discerning. You need to be able to identify the motivations behind your choices and the consequences of those choices.

When you can discern that your motivation is a destructive emotion, you can reframe the situation and make a better decision than if you *couldn't* discern your motivation.

Remember, you'll always be free to think, say, and do whatever you want, but you'll never be free from the consequences of your choices. Conscious people are aware of the choices they make and take responsibility for the consequences.

The Path from Natural to Conscious state is just a question of habit—learn it!

The path that leads natural human beings to become conscious ones looks like this:

Integrality ➔ *Intentionality* ➔ *Coherence* ➔ *Lifelong Learning*

In the integrality step, we need to ask the questions:

- What spheres of my life will this decision impact?
- How will this decision affect the people and environments I will live in in the future?
- How will these changes influence the person I will become?
- How is my past influencing my decisions?
- How much are my decisions being biased by the people and environments in my life (limiting my perspectives)?

With these questions, you're broadening your perspective and identifying systems that can enhance your comprehension of any given situation. Raising your awareness of your integrality this way will help you make more conscious and impactful decisions, acknowledging the stories in your head that are leading to your assumptions, which in turn lead to your choices. It will also help you to identify assumptions that have misled you and course-correct more quickly.

In the intentionality step, we ask:

- What do I want to achieve?
- What do I want in my life?
- What influence do I want to have in others' lives?
- What is the legacy I want to leave?
- What do I want to be remembered for?

By asking these questions, we start to think as intentional beings, raising our consciousness. We begin to make decisions based on what we want rather than what we want to avoid, moving us toward coherence.

In the coherence step, we ask:

- How can I be the same person in all environments I live in?
- How can these different places, systems, and people be a path to what I want in life?
- How can I be myself when the people who surround me change?
- How do I maintain my core wherever I am?
- How do my emotions play a role in my decision-making process, and how do I leverage them to my benefit?

Knowing what we are and what we want is crucial to achieving coherence. People who live intentional lives will be much more authentic than those who don't, given their ability to express their coherence by speaking with clarity about their purpose and who they are.

Finally, we need to adapt, evolve and go with the flow of life. As lifelong learners, we must:

Be aware of all the spheres of our lives and the systems that enter or leave our lives.

Be aware of the stories we're telling ourselves about our lives and about the changes we face. Are these stories blocking or building the future we want to create?

Remind ourselves of what our intentions are and how our purposes evolve based on what we learn from everything we experience.

Always be clear about the person you want to be and what you want from life. No matter how your life evolves, you can be coherent. And be aware that being coherent doesn't mean being stagnant. Learning and changing your opinions and ideas are part of life and evolving and being authentic. That's resilience. The question is how to remain coherent as you change. For those who can do it, the reward is that they can share their purpose and vision with others and inspire them to do the same, creating a coherence flow (We'll talk about this in Chapter 11).

COHERENCE MODEL

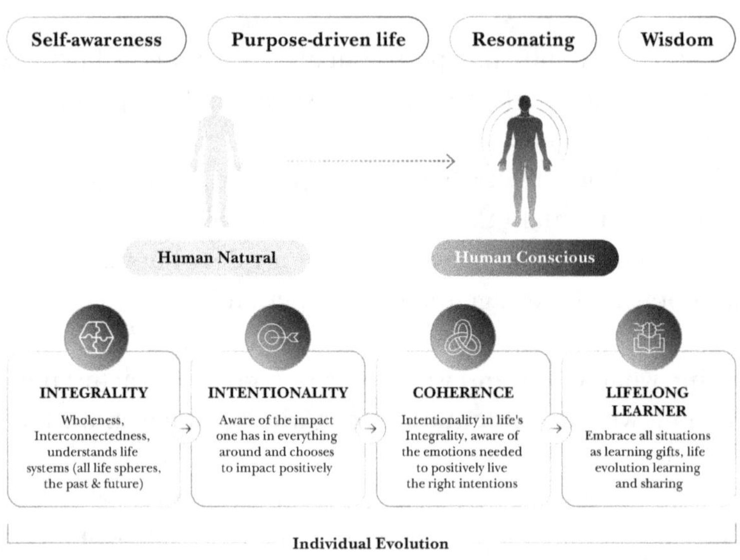

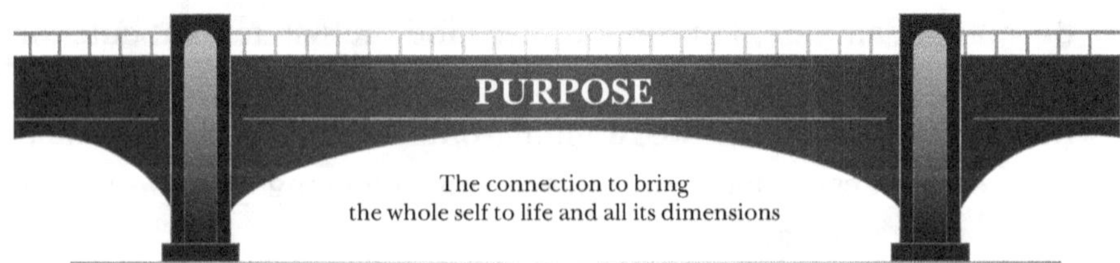

Figure 1

Coherently Living Your Purpose Will Make You an Authentic, Inspiring Leader

Who are the people everyone follows, everyone admires? They're usually people who are consistent and coherent. We recognize them because they live a coherent life and know what they want no matter what challenges emerge. Their message is consistent in all their spheres, and they grow stronger in the face of adversity. As Archbishop Desmond Tutu said, "We have hardship without becoming hard. We have heartbreaks without being broken."

These are the kinds of people we look up to—Archbishop Tutu, Martin Luther King, Gandhi, Nelson Mandela, the Dalai Lama. They all had their struggles but were able to live lives that inspired people and still do. But there are also ordinary people who inspire us because they're clear about what they believe and live their lives accordingly—coherently. In living this way, they provide a clear example for others who want to live the same way.

Some years ago when I went to my thirtieth elementary school reunion, my third-grade teacher told me he always knew I'd be a leader. He reminded me how assertive and clear I was about what I wanted.

"One time, I had to take a medical leave, and the students were informed that a new teacher was going to substitute for me for quite a while," he told me as we sat on the bench beside the old soccer field where he once led our PE classes. "After the announcement, you were so sad and somehow so loyal to me that you felt like it would be a betrayal to like another teacher."

I had no recollection of this.

"All of a sudden, a bunch of the students decided that *they* wouldn't like the new teacher either—because of *you*. So the principal asked me to talk to you and try to change your mind and make you welcome the new teacher properly."

I had to laugh. I couldn't imagine having the power to cause so much commotion at age seven.

"After we talked, you told me, 'Okay, I want to like him now. I'll do this.' And then all the other kids were okay with the new teacher too." He smiled and shook his head. "This is how you were, Lara. Even if you didn't know it, everyone listened to you, and your decisions influenced a lot of the other kids." Pausing, he gave me a wink. "Not always the best way, though."

At that time, I'd just started my position as general manager of Bayer in Hungary and I was a little nervous. But having my former teacher tell me how much I used to influence people and how it didn't always have a positive impact was a helpful reminder. I understood the importance of being intentional in my decisions—intentional about having a positive impact. And I knew that if I had this kind of influence, I could help people. In other words, I knew I could do my job.

From that day on, I made an effort to observe leaders and people in general. Every time I'd arrive in a new country, I'd look for natural leaders, and they were easy to find. They were the ones who were able to speak up and share their thoughts and values. I could always find people who loved to wake up in the morning and loved their jobs, usually because they found meaning in what they were doing. They influenced the whole organization even if they didn't realize it. But the people who inspired me the most were patients and caregivers who believed so strongly in humans' right to good health care that they fought for the cause in addition to holding day jobs, unafraid of being judged or harmed. Today, patient associations led by such mission-driven people are spearheading change in national healthcare policies around the world.

In my thirty years of working as an international executive, I saw many people who were true leaders, inside and outside of corporations and regardless of their titles or positions. Also in that time, my own leadership became very intentional, and although I made many mistakes, my purpose drove me to be a person who would have a positive impact rather than a negative one. And I eventually decided I should try to pass this source of motivation on to my teams.

When you have a clear purpose, you can explain your decisions in a way that makes people understand that they're not selfish decisions. Leaders who do this bring clarity to the world. While not all the world's most influential leaders talk about their purpose, you can be sure they have one. You can tell from their actions—their actions tell us what they're living for. And usually, they're living a life that others admire and want to emulate.

But can just anyone become a leader who inspires and lifts people up? The answer is yes. You don't need to become a spiritual leader like the Dalai Lama. You don't need to be born a minority and overcome daunting prejudices. You just have to be clear about your intentions and consistent about putting the lessons you learn into practice. It takes commitment, but you'll be equipped to face any challenge that comes your way.

It doesn't matter where we're born or what we do for a living; we can all make the choices that will allow us to build the world we want to live in.

When We're Conscious and Intentional, We Create the Future

Everyone can be an inspiring leader. The world has space for us all. The only commonality we all have is that we're unique, and we can all complement each other and make the world a better place.

In 2013, Roche headhunted me after seventeen years with Bayer while I was serving as CEO of the Venezuela operations, and I accepted the offer partly because of the company's leadership approach. Roche ran a more decentralized model, giving local CEOs the freedom to bring their own style and adapt the company's global strategy to each country's market dynamics. Another factor in my decision was the strong focus on people and ethics that I perceived during my "assessment center," a process that evaluates job candidates' skills. During a full-day interaction in Miami, I had to role-play in various scenarios designed to test my ethics and my people-management and decision-making skills. One scenario involved a conversation with a coworker who wasn't performing well after many years of excellent performance, and I kept the conversation professional, avoiding being too soft and compassionate like I usually am. I thought it went well, so the evaluator's comments caught me by surprise: *It was a good conversation,* he wrote, *but you never asked the person how he was feeling, if there was anything going on in his personal life that you could help him with or that could help you understand his recent behavior.*

That was it. This was the company where I knew I could make a difference as the leader I always wanted to be. For some years, my leadership had a clear intention: I wanted to bring spirituality to the workplace, and I wanted others to reach their full potential through their love for what they were doing. And working for Roche would allow me to have the greatest possible impact for patients around the world and bring the greatest benefit to the company.

Four years later, I got the opportunity to implement my leadership style even more fully. I'd always hoped to work in India someday, and in 2017 my wish came true when Roche transferred me there. A significant part of my studies had been based on ancient Indian wisdom, and I knew my leadership philosophy would be easily understood there.

After a month spent learning the business with the leadership team in Mumbai, though, it was time for my first town hall meeting, and the communication director told me that my plan to open it with some of the "hug therapy" I'd introduced in Venezuela might be a tough sell. Personal life and professional life never mix in Indian culture, let alone in the corporate realm, and public displays of affection are rare. But she said that if I felt strongly about it, I should give it a shot. So I gave it a shot.

"Before we start, I want to ask you all to do something that is very important to me," I said. "Shilpika advised me that it might not be the best the way to start because she's very respectful of your privacy, but I want to give it a try. I want to ask everybody to start with hug therapy. Of course, if any of you don't feel comfortable with it, that's super-okay. For the rest of you, let's just hug each other to show our appreciation and care."

And guess what? After a couple of minutes, I had to shout into the microphone to get them to stop hugging and expressing their appreciation. It worked! (Hug therapy went on to become a tradition for us, just like in Venezuela.)

Next task: spark enthusiasm for our purpose. The most recent survey indicated that the team members' engagement was very low; 40 percent reported that they were unhappy at work and weren't committed to staying with the company, meaning we were at risk of losing our workforce at any moment. They saw their jobs as a burden and an obligation, and I needed to change that.

When I had their attention again after all the hugging, I told them what my intentions were.

"I'm here to make the business work, but beyond this, when I leave, I'll know whether I've been successful based on whether I've built a workplace where you want to be and feel good about. I want you to wake up in the morning smiling and feeling grateful because you're doing what you want to do with your lives. I want as many patients to be treated as possible, not just because of the financial results but also because each of us has to be proud of what we're doing. I want all of you to love your work as I love mine."

By the end of the meeting, I felt supported by the whole organization. Many of the team members came up to me to offer their help and ask how they could be part of what was emerging. It was the start of a wonderful relationship with the team and a moment I still have in my heart.

In the months that followed, the leadership team implemented a new strategy and operating model that allowed room for feelings and emotions in the workplace and established a new mission based on Roche's global purpose: *Doing Now What Patients Need Next.* The vision extended beyond selling medicines to supporting projects nationwide to improve the healthcare system around the country. After two years, the team changed my title from chief executive officer to chief purpose officer, and the local newspaper, *The Mint*, published a story about my leadership style with the headline "A new-age leader's office mantra: Hugs, yoga, and fines for calling her Ma'am." Meanwhile, *Forbes* called me out for being the first world's CEO to give up that title to be a chief purpose officer instead.

When I stepped down from my position after two years, the *Mumbai*

Mirror wrote, "Lara Bezerra has transformed leadership in the pharmaceutical industry forever." But it wasn't me—it was the potential that had been unleashed and the team members' effort to live their purpose through the common purpose of the company. Although I led the team, our shared belief was what inspired the Indian pharmaceutical market to become more collaborative, proactive, and patient-focused, unleashing its true essence. The team members had learned to live coherently, guided by their purpose.

Today, many who worked with me in India tell me they're still guided by that purpose. They still hold in their hearts the importance of seeing the whole instead of pieces and collaborating at a level that transcends numbers and even their own conscious ambitions.

We can all be inspiring leaders when we understand the impact our intentions have. We can show others how to lead coherent lives and, when they have a shared purpose, how to collaborate in a way that yields solutions in the blink of an eye. Remember how waves can grow much bigger and to a much higher wavelength when they enter resonance? When we're collectively aware of what each other wants in life and resonate with each other, we can advance human consciousness. This is collaboration at the highest level.

Every one of us is a leader at a certain point in our lives. Knowing the power of our purpose and employing effective communication can open doors we never imagined we could. Often, just sharing our dreams and purpose awakens people to possibilities they didn't see before, and that's how the biggest transformations start.

Consider the story of Mahatma Gandhi. Although he was shy and struggled academically, he came from a family with strong values and had a strong belief in justice and nonviolence and a deep respect for diversity. While studying law in London, he took his first step toward leadership by joining the London Vegetarian Society as a member of the executive committee. Later, upon witnessing the disenfranchisement of Indians in South Africa, where he was working as a **lawyer** for a merchant firm, he chose to stay and fight for his community's rights rather than return to safety in India. For seven years, he spearheaded nonviolent protests against the South African government. Ultimately, their unwavering commitment led to concessions that improved the lives of Indians in South Africa.

Gandhi's experiences in South Africa were transformative. He didn't succumb to initial challenges but drew strength from his upbringing, transforming his shyness and self-doubt into unwavering self-belief. He embraced the principles of nonviolence and respect as the core of his leadership philosophy. While his impact in South Africa may not have been as monumental as that of figures like Desmond Tutu and Nelson Mandela, the lessons learned there would become crucial for his future fight for India's independence. What's more, he unknowingly awakened a spirit of leadership and resilience within South Africa's Indian community, a quality he would later inspire on a much larger scale in his home country.

Gandhi reframed what could have been a very ordinary life dictated by circumstances into the life of an inspiring leader. He transformed the suffering of past relationships and environments into powerful tools for transforming millions of people, both during his life and after he died. By sending a clear message of what he wanted for himself and his future, he inspired Mandela, Martin Luther King and many others to become leaders as inspiring as he was.

That's how we create inspiring leaders, by setting an example for others to follow. And the first step in setting that example is integrality. In Chapter Four, we'll take that first step down the path to consciousness and all its benefits.

PART TWO

THE FOUR PILLARS OF COHERENCE

PILLAR ONE

INTEGRALITY

CHAPTER 4

THE UNIVERSE CAN CONSPIRE IN OUR FAVOR

The Power of Integrality

It's easier to live in coherence when we see our life in connection with everything that impacts it. Past, present and future are part of this impact, and so are the relationships and environments we're part of. Several systems are in play around us, each having a life of its own in addition to their collective life together. We can help the universe to conspire in our favor when we're aware of the spheres of our lives and act consciously in all of them, not afraid to express our wishes and dreams. This is seeing the integrality of our lives and acting on it.

INTEGRALITY

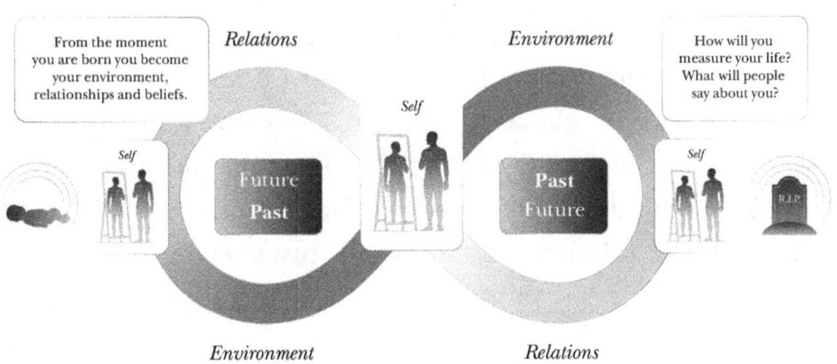

Figure 2

As a young adult, I had no problem sharing my life with others, and I was often advised to keep my greatest ambitions to myself. (In Brazil, this is common advice for protecting yourself against the jealousy of those who aren't as self-confident as you might be.) But that didn't feel right to me. I thought that the more we talk about our plans, the easier they'll be to achieve, and the more likely the universe would be to send help our way. But one day I didn't feel like acting as I believed. I felt like hiding my life.

While I was reading about Yoga philosophy and practicing physical yoga during my time as general manager at Bayer Pharma in Hungary in my early thirties, I learned that life is much more than working and having a family. But two years into my time there, I was still struggling to bring work and family into harmony with the other facets of my life.

During a weekend yoga retreat, the Saturday dinner conversation was about corporations' negative impact on society, including pharmaceutical companies. How could someone support the greed of the pharma industry? As the conversation went on, I tried to get smaller and smaller, hiding as much of my six-foot-one frame as possible. I knew they were right to a degree, but that wasn't the whole truth. I was proud to work for the pharma industry. But that didn't stop me from grabbing my things in the middle of the night and going right back home. I couldn't bring myself to lie about my job, but I also didn't have the energy to defend it. This weekend was supposed to be about making myself stronger, more spiritual, and a better human being.

In the following weeks, the fact that I hadn't been true to myself haunted me. I considered leaving the pharma industry, moving to another country, and starting a new life focused on spiritual growth and teachings. When I told my mother about this, she argued that it would be the easy path. I'd be avoiding the hardship of evolving my spirituality in the place where it was needed the most. Leaving the corporation wouldn't make corporations disappear; the only thing I'd be achieving was walking away from a system I believed wasn't living its essence. Instead, I could remain part of it and live my purpose by helping it to live *its* purpose: to benefit society and make life better for humanity.

On that day, I decided to remain as part of the system and make it better instead of taking the easy way out. In fact, I took a step back and observed *all* the systems I was part of and considered how I could make them resonate with my belief. I shifted my focus from pursuing a work-life balance to pursuing an overall *life* balance. Rather than trying to dedicate the same amount of time to all the separate parts of my life, I'd integrate all those parts toward my purpose. And before I knew it, my dilemma about whether to prioritize my personal life or my professional life resolved. For several years, I'd delayed planning a family for the sake of my career, but now I decided to go for both instead of either-or, and I believed I could do it if I sought spiritual growth in whichever system I happened to be operating in at any given time. So I connected my past, present, and future and my personal and professional lives with that single focus. I decided to live my spirituality at work.

The idea of somehow separating work from life would mean that when we're working we aren't living, and that's impossible. Being alive means we're always working, as partners, parents, citizens, and professionals. If we separate those roles from each other, we'll never be able to find true harmony. By changing our focus to bring the right intention to all the systems we belong to, we can achieve that harmony, living in greater coherence and finding more balance in our lives. Knowing the importance of the connections among our systems and how they affect our life gives us the power to use them as tools to fulfill our purpose.

When we understand the systems we're part of, it's easier to live in coherence, and life becomes interesting and challenging instead of overwhelming. But just how can we understand the systems we're part of?

We Are Because of Our Interactions

When clients and I explore their purpose during my mentoring sessions, I employ exercises to encourage them to reflect on their lives. In one exercise, I ask them to imagine that they're at their own funerals:

"You've died happy and satisfied with the life you lived. You're proud of your choices and impact in the world. You're observing the room, and in one corner friends, colleagues, parents, and other fellow community members are smiling and talking about you. They're sharing how you lived a happy life and how you've made a lasting impact on *their* lives. They all describe you similarly because you lived coherently and you were yourself: authentic, vulnerable, and always certain of what you wanted. You lived your purpose, and they could tell it."

Then I ask the following questions:

- How are they describing you?
- To what actions do they attribute their impressions of you?
- How are they describing your behavior with them?
- When they're asked about your purpose in life, what do they answer?

Then I ask, "If today were the last day of your life, what would these same people say about you?" Here I'm asking them to look at their lives until today. What have their choices been? How have they made decisions? How have they behaved? How do their choices and behavior impact others today? Would others talk about them as they'd like them to?

- How would they describe you?
- What impression did you leave on them with your last interactions?
- How would they describe your behavior with them?
- How would they describe you in your professional life?
- When asked about your purpose in life, what would they answer?

Finally, I ask them to compare answers and consider what they have to do now to be remembered the way they want to be remembered at their funeral:

- How can you show up as the same person in all parts of your life, the person you want to be remembered as?

- Is there any place in your life where you should change your behavior?
- How can you leverage your purpose in all the systems of your life?

In doing this exercise, people start to understand that for others to remember them a certain way in life, they have to *behave* that way. This sounds obvious, but I assure you that few people realize this and have already made the decision to live an intentional life.

Many thinkers talk about interdependence and systems-thinking in the new world that's unfolding. Interdependence is one of the commonalities between science and spiritual belief systems such as Buddhism, Hinduism, Sufism, and Kabbalah. What's known as *entanglement* in quantum physics is called *connectedness* in spirituality—the energy that brings all the universe into existence. A flower can't exist without the sun, water or soil. The sun and the soil couldn't exist without the other elements in the universe. We as human beings *are* because of our interactions with the elements and with other humans. And depending on how all the aspects our lives change—climate, air, water, families, work—or how we interpret the change, *we* will change. And how we change—what we become—will influence the same elements that influenced us yesterday.

If we know we're becoming our interpretation of our relationships and our environments and we're conscious of what we want in life, external factors will have less impact on our future and we'll be able to make better decisions—decisions that lead to the kind of constructive experiences we want to have. In my case, I almost became a consequence of the guilt I felt at the yoga retreat, but because my mother helped me reflect on what I really wanted and where I could have the most impact, I became a different person. She guided me to reframe my interpretation of my past, seeing that moment of guilt and doubt as a good thing. As a result, I decided to remain in the corporate world. Instead of fighting against my guilt with the same anger and aversion that *created* the guilt or simply running away from it in search of an easier, more peaceful life, I drew on love and compassion to live a life where I would bring spirituality and purpose to corporations and the people who are part of them. This reframed my future in light of my emerging purpose, and I was no longer living in a world I despised because of others' opinions. Instead, I was part of something I admired and was helping to create. Instead of leaving and fighting the system, I'd decided to become part of the system and change it.

The Dalai Lama received the Nobel Peace Prize for his concept of universal responsibility, which is a product of his belief in the interdependence of the universe. Simply put, universal responsibility is our responsibility for anything and everything that's unfolding in our universe. Every one of our thoughts, words, and actions influences something in our universe, and this in turn influences who we are and our future. To understand that we have this power is to understand integrality.

We Can Integrate Everything

Consider your past, present, and future—your entire life span. Can you live free from the limitations created by the ghosts of your past and by your plans and expectations for the future? Is your past a flexible block you're molding into the right foundation for all your hopes and dreams?

Consider your relationships and your environment, the boundless connections among nature, people, and planet. The environment and the people around us have great influence on our lives, from the place where we're born to the people who raise us to the places where we choose to live. Our contact with these people and place creates our personalities, regardless of our genes. But what would happen if you weren't limited by the boundaries of place and relationships? Can you look beyond these limitations and see the infinite possibilities and opportunities? Can you recognize the potential of the universe you were born into instead of the limitations of the ego you developed? I can either see myself as "only" Lara, born in São Paulo, Brazil, daughter, sister, with the limited possibilities offered by my parents and my environment, or see myself as a citizen of the planet, part of an infinite universe, who's free to choose the places and people in her life and how they affect her on the way to becoming what she wants to be remembered for.

When we separate parts of life or segregate our past from our present or future rather than embracing the wholeness of our existence, we only have a partial view. We only get some of the information we need to make good decisions, and we *are* our decisions. If I'd decided to search for a work-life balance when I was young and blamed myself for loving my work in the pharmaceutical industry, this might have led me to stay in my country with my family and I wouldn't have met my husband in Mexico and our kids in Venezuela. My work brought me my personal life. Our hearts and minds know the balance we need to search for in life—they know what we want to be remembered for when we're gone. And if we let our hearts and minds guide us and live with our purpose in mind, decisions will be easier and coherent and we won't separate the dimensions of our lives. We'll be able to live as one, all the parts of our lives connected by the purpose we want to live and the person we want to become.

In the story in Chapter 3 about the young Brazilian politician Arthur Do Val, he thought he could separate his benevolent public image from his less charitable private side. But life showed him that he's one wherever he is and that whatever he decides to be in any area of his life will spill into the other areas—all the systems connected to his life. I thought I could run away from my doubts by changing jobs and giving up my career, but my mother showed me how I could acknowledge all the systems of my life, and instead of walking away from something that appeared to be an obstacle in my life (working for a corporation), I decided to make the obstacle my vehicle for spreading the spirituality I believed in. I leveraged the interdependence of the systems in my life.

Both these examples show how connected our environment and relationships are. If Do Val were the same person in private as he was in public, he would have been a more effective politician—the politician he aspired to be. The more we leverage the systems around us and the connections among them, the easier life is.

And the more systems we have in life, the more important it is for us to review our purpose and consider how we might want to change it in light of the new possibilities life has presented us. A reevaluation of Do Val's system might have made him want to inspire his friends to aid him in his journey to help people and countries in need instead of continuing to embrace the mindset of a younger, more irresponsible self. The more conscious we become, the more cognitively mature we become.

Being aware of the new systems that enter our lives and how they can transform the previous ones allows us to add more power to our purpose. In the next chapter, we'll see how

CHAPTER 5

WE ARE SYSTEMS WITHIN SYSTEMS

PRACTICING INTEGRALITY

"You are not just a drop in the ocean; you are the entire ocean."
—Rumi

As more systems are added to your life on the way to adulthood, your integrality becomes more complex. The decision-making process requires more input, and you need to be open to others' views and increase your awareness about the role of all systems in your life. The more openly you listen to others and observe through others' eyes, the more comprehensive *your* view will be and the more information you'll have in making decisions. When you understand your impact and how your choices will change the future, you can make better decisions.

My first relationships were with my Japanese mother and my Brazilian father, both medical doctors, and my grandparents, and later came my brother and sister. My environment was my family. When we moved to a large condominium complex, I entered a Japanese kindergarten and now my environment also included my class and the condo community, and my relationships encompassed friends and new authority figures—teachers. As I grew up, swimming, ballet, and school all added new systems to my life. Most of them were chosen for me, although choices such as who to befriend and which sports to play were mine. At the age of sixteen, I suddenly had to make a choice that was going to determine the course of my life: what college to attend. Did I have enough information or the necessary maturity to make the best possible decision? Of course not, but the way my parents raised me and the challenges I faced during my first sixteen years helped me make what I considered to be a good decision. Between my parents' divorce and the typical drama that a teenage girl has to endure, I was ready for something less involved than medical school, which had been my original choice, and I decided to go to business school. It was shorter and I could make money faster, allowing me to get on with my life sooner. Once I was in college, my parents' example factored in to my decision to seek an internship in the pharmaceutical industry. And because my parents' dedication to whatever they did and my father's leisure hours spent reading *The Lancet* or the *New England Journal of Medicine* had led me to think of working as a natural and pleasant part of life rather than an obligation separated from the rest of life, I chose to hold down a job when I wasn't attending classes in order to pay for my studies.

As the years passed, the systems I became part of—relationships with friends, boyfriends, their families, college, more sports—added more complexity to my life. And my passion for my studies, sports and healthy living led me to relationships and environments that helped me to become cognitively mature and develop habits like self-discipline that would lead to good decisions in some tough situations.

When I was twenty-nine, I'd been working in the pharma industry for six years and was invited to go to Portugal as an expatriate. But six months before I was supposed to depart, my mother had an aortic rupture that a doctor said wouldn't allow her to live more than another year. A few weeks after she was back at home, we were having breakfast together and I told her I wouldn't leave Brazil because I wanted to stay with her.

She gave me a warm smile. "Does this mean your future depends on how fast I die?"

Oh my God—what are you saying?

"If you stay, I'll have to wish for my death as soon as possible so you can live the life you deserve," she said. "But if you leave, I'll have every reason to stay alive and visit you."

I left for Portugal six months later, and over the next six years my mother came to visit me there and in Germany, where I took subsequent positions.

Thanks to my mother's decision-making abilities, which were based on focusing on what we want and seeing the opportunities in everything, I hadn't allowed the increasing complexity of my life to overwhelm my own decision-making abilities, and it gave me six more years of time with her.

I also hadn't let it cost me important career opportunities—opportunities that she very much wanted for me—or the connections to new systems that came with them. Each new country brought a whole new system into my life, new relationships and environments I had to integrate fast. My positions brought me into contact with governments and various public officials, and always being the same person and not wearing different masks in different situations helped me navigate the network of ministers, ambassadors, yoga teachers, colleagues, family members, and friends that my environment now encompassed. Thanks to my mother's guidance, I had the opportunity to pursue my dream to inspire policymakers and influential citizens in various countries to do better by their societies and humanity in general, even if it was only by planting a seed with a single colleague.

Living abroad also gave me a better understanding of how countries work together and influence each other. I got to see a level of interdependence we normally don't see when we spend our whole lives in one country. But now, thanks to technology, there's an open flow of information about all of this, and we all have the opportunity to be more aware of the systems we're part of.

How aware are you of this complexity of life and the systems you're part of? Do you know the right systems to join, the ones that will best allow you to serve your purpose? Are you letting life decide for you, or are you deciding your life?

Every Choice Matters

It's important to choose well when deciding where to be and who to spend your time with. As Jim Rohn, author of *The Art of Extraordinary Living,* says, "We're the average of the five people we spend the most time with." The friendships and the places you choose will drive your life. For example, if your friends love fast food and sweets and their weekend hobby is trying new fast-food chains, it won't matter if you'd prefer to be eating healthily—you'll be trapped by your friends' decisions and this environment you've chosen.

It's important to be aware of *all* the choices we make, even small ones. Absolutely everything we choose will have a consequence in our future. How many times have we made a choice on autopilot, not giving the proper importance to the situation, and we're later caught by surprise when people "help" us in a way that's completely different from what we wanted because of their assumptions based on our autopilot's decision? In Buddhism the term *karma* means exactly this. Any decision you make, whether intentional or not, will have a positive or a negative effect on what we're becoming.

One day my son came home and told me he was going to compete in the breaststroke for the high school swim team despite liking the butterfly more. When I asked his coach about it, he said my son should swim the breaststroke.

"Whenever I ask him to swim whatever he wants, he chooses breast, maybe because at that moment he chooses what's easier for him. As a result, he's becoming very good at breaststroke, better than he is at butterfly, and I have to choose what fits the team best. In his case, he's training more on breaststroke, so guess why he's swimming breaststroke?"

When I went back to my son, I asked him what style he really wanted to swim.

"Butterfly," he said without hesitation.

"Then what's the style you have to choose whenever you're given a choice?"

"Butterfly?!"

We both burst out laughing. The exchange reminded us of a lesson from a course my kids took when they were eight or nine, "Spirituality for Kids," which asked them to reflect on whether they wanted instant happiness or true plenitude. After this, he made decisions based on what he really wanted, and not just about swimming.

We often make decisions without thinking, just reacting to the moment and what it brings. If we aren't conscious, we're just passive victims of circumstance and reactive emotions. But if we just ask the simple question "What do I really want?" we're on our way to making more conscious decisions and finding the systems where we belong.

Integrality - Getting to know our systems is the first step in influencing them

The following exercise can help you start the journey to coherence by identifying systems you might not realize you're part of that have an impact on your life and the person you're becoming. Reflect on them from time to time and you'll become much more intentional in the decision-making that demonstrates your integrality.

Exercise 1 – Knowing Your Systems – Environments & People: What I Am Becoming

Environment:

List the places where you spend most of your time. Beside each place, list the two or three biggest influences it has on your life. Then answer the following questions:

- Is this what you want in your life?
- If yes, how can you enhance your environment's influence on you?
- If not, can you change how it influences you?
- If so, how?
- If you can't change how it influences you, what can you do to influence the environment?

- How do you stay aware of what's going on in the world?
- Do you vote?
- Do you know why you work where you do?
- Do you know why you live where you do?
- Do you know why you eat and buy what you do?
- How do you decide what to read?
- Do you know how to get your social media algorithm to bring you more diverse information than what you're currently getting?
- How much does what's going on in the world impact you?
- Can you be aware of what's going in the world and still stay in your core?

In the following table, build your decision-making matrix to select environments that will be a better fit for you than your current environments. If you can't change an environment, you'll learn how to make it your training field for developing strength and resilience.

Places I spend the most time	Biggest influences they have on my life	Is this what I want in my life?	If yes, how can I enhance their influences?	If not, can I change how they influence me? How?	If I can't change how they influence me, what can I do to change the environment?

Relationships:

List the people you spend the most time with. Beside their names, list the two or three biggest effects they've had on your life. Then answer the following questions:

- Are these effects what you want in your life?
- If yes, how can you enhance their impact?
- If not, can you change how they affect you?
- If so, how?
- If you can't change how they affect your life, what can you do to change the relationships?
- Do you know why you have the friends you have?
- Where could you meet new people who will add more light to your life?
- What new people could you follow on social media?
- Who could you contact to talk about topics of interest to you? Make a list.
- Is there somebody you find especially interesting and have always wanted to meet? Write to the person.
- Is there anybody from your past who had a strong positive influence on your life you'd like to bring back into your life? Write to the person.

People I spend the most time with	Biggest impacts they've had on my life	Is this what I want in my life?	If yes, how can I enhance their impact?	If not, can I change how they impact me? How?	If I can't change how they impact me, what can I do to change the relationship?

Your Purpose Helps You to Integrate Past, Present, and Future

Your past is the building block of your present and your future. And it's the result of all the decisions you've made, some good and some not so good. But in a sense, your future also determines your past. How? If you have a dream, a clear plan for the future, it will determine what you *make* of your past. Which experiences will you consciously build on as you build your present and future? Which lessons will you take to heart? If you *don't* have dreams or a purpose, you *are* your past, limited by your past experiences and the way you've processed them. Negative experiences will be the main determinant of your present, becoming a filter for anything that happens and creating a negative bias in your life, and this bias will be the decision-making filter that determines who you become. But if you have a clear purpose, *that* will become your filter, and you'll be more likely to learn from experiences so that they serve your purpose. Having a purpose helps you integrate past, present, and future, and this integrality will bring coherence to your life, allowing you to have a constructive perspective of your past.

In building yourself, you also need to use the filters of the present and the future. The present represents the chance to make conscious decisions and analyze what your past taught you and what you want from your future. The future represents the infinite possibility of realizing dreams, being a better person and aiming for happiness and fulfillment. Both are very important considerations, right?

In Japanese culture, the concepts of *wabi-sabi* and *kintsugi* have to do with how we observe the past and the imperfections of our lives. Rather than finding fault in the things that go "wrong," *wabi-sabi* (侘寂) encourages us to appreciate that nothing is truly perfect or permanent. The reframing of past imperfections is key to building the future we want. And that's where the concept of *kintsugi* (金継ぎ) comes in. Literally "golden" (*kin*) and "repair" (*tsugi*), it's an art that glues pieces of broken pottery together with liquid gold or silver, and the result is something more beautiful than it was before it was broken.

This is how life works. The past is past, but you can reframe mistakes in a way that transforms your life into something more beautiful than it would be if it weren't for those "mistakes."

When I was undergoing my third in vitro fertilization treatment in 2009, I was sure I was going to get pregnant. I'd spent a year suffering and regretting not being able to conceive naturally, and another year bouncing from Mexico to Peru to Brazil, and it was time. As I told the doctor, I had things all scheduled out, and this was the place in the schedule where I needed to get pregnant.

He smiled. "Lara, in this particular field of life, business logic and strategy won't work. It doesn't matter how organized and professional you are. Executives like you are used to getting things done and getting what they want, but in this case it's not under your control. You need to have patience and wisdom. Intelligence won't work."

Two years later, after three in-vitro failures, he turned out to be right. Intelligence hadn't worked. Apparently, there was no place for logic and strategy in conception.

Back in Mexico, I was trying to decide what to do next when my father got me thinking during a phone conversation. "Daughter, you are so intelligent," he said. "You make such conscious decisions at work. But I can't understand you now. Do you want to get pregnant or do you want to be a mother?"

"Of course, a mother." *But they're the same thing.*

"Well, if you keep insisting on getting pregnant, you might not be here to take care of your child."

Finally, a few months later, I got it. Being a mother is about raising kids, not giving birth to them. If I insisted on trying in-vitro again, I'd be flooding my body once more with powerful hormones that can swell the ovaries, damage the heart, and drain the spirit, and I'd have sacrificed my life for the wrong goal. So my husband and I decided to adopt instead. But after years of being unable to adopt in Brazil because I'd been transferred to Venezuela and there was not an adoption agreement between the countries, we finally accepted the fact that we weren't going to be parents. To try to fill the void, we planned to create an institution to focus on helping children around the world. And serving as executive president of Bayer, I focused on my work so much that the fact that we hadn't been able to adopt stopped hurting so much.

Two years later, though, I accepted the position as CEO of Roche's Venezuelan affiliate, and within a few months an "angel" in the organization, Mariela Ball, suggested my husband and I go to a foundation called Fundana to find out about its adoption process. My husband was receptive to the idea, eager even.

"If we tried for so long and it never happened, maybe it just wasn't the right time," he said. "We should go, right? Even if all the circumstances tell us not to, we should, right?"

We decided to look at the past as a lesson and not as a hurdle. If we'd focused on all the pain and suffering we endured, we probably would have tried to avoid going through it all again and we wouldn't have accepted this gift. But we saw it as a sign that our children were already waiting for us.

Long story short, it was the best decision of our lives. In August 2013 we met our three children— Marco, eight, Sara, six, and Lily, five— and since then we've been the happiest parents on earth. We now see my infertility as a blessing, and I remember my suffering as the worst possible waste of energy. My children were waiting for me, but I was insisting on a road that wasn't mine.

When things don't happen as planned, it's only because what you need is waiting for you somewhere else. You're just stuck on a path that isn't the right one. My painful past was a building block for the love and gratitude and happiness I now feel as a mother. My "soul pregnancy"—the time when I was attempting in-vitro—lasted three years because that's how long I needed to prepare myself for the "birth" of my children.

Now I live life conscious of the fact that each situation is a stepping-stone. When I start to suffer because something isn't according to my plans, I take a step back. *Okay, this plan didn't work, but it's not about the plan—it's about my dream. What did I really want when I came up with this plan?* I didn't get pregnant, but why did I want to get pregnant in the first place? Because I wanted to be a mom, to build a family. And I eventually came to see that there was another way of getting what I wanted.

When I ask myself what I want but don't know the answer, I recall some advice my mother gave me: "Not having an answer is also an answer. Waiting is important for you to arrive at the right moment, the right time for things to flow. In the end, everything is going to be okay. If it's not okay now, wait—it's not the end yet."

Just as you can reframe your past by asking yourself what you really wanted, you can reframe your decisions about the future the same way. When I told my mother I wouldn't move to Portugal because I didn't want to miss her last months of life, she reframed my future by making me see what I really wanted. Basing such a decision on what I *didn't* want wouldn't make either of us happy. I didn't want her to die while I was far away from her, but that wouldn't prevent her from dying, and in the meantime, she'd feel bad about every year that passed that I wasn't living my dream. She made me see that living my dream would give her the strength to live and come visit me. And that's exactly how it worked out. Over the next six years, my mother visited me in Portugal, Germany and Hungary before passing in 2006.

As they say, be careful what you wish for. If you don't wish for what you really want and live with this intention always in mind—coherently—your life story is likely to have an unhappy ending.

Exercise 2 – My Past and Who I Became – Positive Reframing of My Story

---

Imagine you're writing the book of your life.

- List the three or four events of the past that had the most influence/impact on your life.
- Describe why each was a good or bad experience.
- Write one sentence about how each good experience has affected who you are today.

- List the lessons you learned from the bad experiences and explain how they've helped you build the person you want to be.

All of us have a story of our lives we tell ourselves and others when we're trying to define who we are at a deep level. Write a short paragraph telling the story of your life through the events you've identified as being the most impactful in your life. Describe how, whether the experience was bad or good, each one positively affected who you are and shaped your dreams. This story will help you to know who you are and build yourself as an authentic person, not despite what's happened to you, but *because* of what's happened to you. In time, you'll learn that you don't need to avoid any part of your life and that telling your story rather than hiding it will help others understand you and encourage them to help you achieve your dreams.

Past events	Good or bad experience?	Why?	If it was good, write one sentence about the impact on who you are today	If it was bad, list a lesson learned from it	If it was bad, how did it help build the person you want to be?

Being Coherent Can Make the Difference between Failure and Success

During my Venezuela assignment with Roche, the country was experiencing extreme economic and political challenges. There was a horizon of scarcity and a possible impediment to importing medicines, creating a need to strategize about communication with stakeholders, and the team would have to figure out the best solution. Among the directors, many discussions about how to react were taking place, as well as how to "protect" and spare our people from the dire situation we were facing until it became necessary to tell them. But I was having trouble with the concept of hiding information from the team. What if we had to implement some extreme strategy? We'd have to take time to prep the team first. If they were with us from the beginning, though, they might help us in making a decision.

Eventually, we hired a consultant to help us think clearly and objectively about our options. I opened the meeting by reading a passage from the *Bhagavad Gita* that I hoped would set the tone. It was about making decisions not based in fear, being transparent, and always doing what's ultimately the best for our purpose. In our case, the purpose was to help patients and the country, and as it turned out, the strategy we decided on was to be completely transparent about the situation, not only with our people but with *everyone*: patients, medical students and the government.

The message we wanted to send was "We're here for the country and for patients." Many other companies had already withdrawn from the country or reduced their portfolios significantly, but we wanted to keep the company in the country for as long as possible. If we couldn't import our products anymore, we'd figure out the minimum portfolio of products we could bring in that would allow us to stay in the country until it recovered and we could resume imports. And this strategy was conveyed to everyone.

We started a crisis room where we met every Monday to monitor the situation and check on the status of our stock, what imports were included in the emergency plan we'd devised, and what imports the government had approved (at the time, the government was our main client). We'd then pass this information on to our whole organization and all stakeholders. As a result, government officials, patient associations, and physicians from the various specialties we worked with started to work together to try to minimize the impact of the lack of products on patients.

When the worst-case scenario came to pass, we no longer had authorization to import and had to put our commercialization on hold. We were terrified of what the reaction would be from the medical community, especially patients, but ultimately we believed we owed it to physicians and patients to inform them of the situation immediately so they had as much time as possible to make other arrangements to obtain medications. We couldn't just let doctors wake up one day and find that the meds they needed for their patients weren't available.

Right after that week's Monday meeting, we called a meeting with the entire company to inform everybody of the situation. Initially, the whole team was afraid of the transparency strategy, but after a couple of weeks, their reaction was unanimously positive. They genuinely appreciated our honesty, and many of them appreciated the courage we'd shown.

We were prepared for the worst because they all knew a restructuring would have to come and sales jobs would be cut, but an amazing thing happened. Rather than asking about their jobs, they expressed their commitment to the company. They knew that whatever we were doing was in the best interest of the patients and the country. And it only happened because they'd been part of the devising of our strategy. Being involved from the beginning created a sense of commitment and responsibility among the team that paid off, as they were our strongest support net until the moment we had to implement the restructuring.

Unfortunately, the team's supportive stance didn't make it any easier when the time came to announce the cuts. On the day we would announce the restructuring, we invited the whole sales force to Caracas for the weekend. During dinner the evening before the announcement was to be made, I shared the situation with my family, and they declared a "red alert." I always share difficult developments with them because some days I really need their support, and on the hardest days the kids issue red alerts as a signal to each other that one of us need hugs immediately. And that's what they did on this day, gathered around me at the dining room table.

Later that night, I got a call from one of the sales-team leaders. "Lara, we know what will happen tomorrow," she said. "We can't imagine how you and the other directors are feeling. We guessed what's going to happen, and we brought the company laptops and other belongings to give back and help HR. I want to thank you for everything you've done and all your efforts to help our country and us."

I was so moved that all I could say was "Thank you" before hanging up so she wouldn't hear me sobbing.

The next morning, I got up before dawn so I could get to the office before everyone else. As I headed through the hall leading to our garage around five thirty, I noticed a small figure sitting in the dark on the bench along the wall. When she stood up, I could see that it was my eight-year-old daughter.

Sasa reached up to hug me. "Mom, everything will be okay," she said as I held her. "You did right. You're a good person."

Somehow, I felt a surge of strength. "Thank you, sweetheart."

As it turned out, it was one of the hardest days of my life, but not as hard as it would have been if I'd kept my turmoil to myself and hadn't let my family come to my rescue.

A couple of days later, I was driving to work when the medical director called me from the office and told me to turn on the radio because some of the patients taking our medicines and their parents were being interviewed. When I tuned in, the host of the program was talking about how badly these families were being affected by the lack of medicines, and then he asked one of the parents to tell his story. He explained that one of our products had been helping his son live a normal life and that without it his condition was quickly deteriorating. After he started to cry, the host of the program began to criticize the company that imported the medicine—us. But the father interrupted him.

"The company has done everything it could," he said, regaining his composure. "I was informed of everything they tried to do to import the medicine for my son. I know they did their best."

Then other patients spoke up to confirm our efforts to help them.

Suddenly, I heard sobs coming from the phone, which I hadn't hung up. Everyone at the office was listening to the interview too, and it sounded like they were overcome by their concern for the patients. After all, we were in this business to help them, and it was hard not to feel like we'd let them down even though we did everything we could for them.

Ultimately, I'm proud of the effort we made. I believe we handled an impossible situation the best way possible: with full transparency and a coherent message. And I'm sure that many of our team members learned something very valuable: that being ourselves, working and living with our purpose in mind, and being coherent wherever we are can make the difference between failure and success when we have to make difficult choices. As my mother used to tell me, time is the best friend of good people and good decisions and the worst enemy of bad people and bad decisions. Time will tell who decided well and who decided poorly—there's no hiding it.

My doubts and fears in Venezuela could have created limiting beliefs and a limiting life, but because of the environment I'd chosen to live in, the people I'd surrounded myself with, and how I saw my past and future, my experience in Venezuela was the richest I'd ever had, in terms of both my personal and professional life. I left Venezuela as a leader I knew I would always be proud of and with the family I'd dreamed of.

These are the kinds of choices that determine our future and the person we become. How we show up for life is our choice, and we can live it consciously and intentionally. And it becomes easier as it becomes part of us.

PILLAR TWO

INTENTIONALITY

CHAPTER 6

WE CAN CHOOSE HOW WE LIVE

The Power and Practice of Intentionality

When I was a teen, I had strong mood swings and, like any teen, moments when my temper got away from me. I complained about everything. Whenever something would go differently from what I planned, different from how I expected it to go, I'd get very frustrated. I only wanted to be happy—why did things keep getting in the way?

Whenever I whined, my mother asked me, "Lara, do you want to be happy?"

"Yes, of course," I'd say. "That's *exactly* what I want."

"Then be it!"

As simple as that. If you want something to happen, then you need to live the right intention. That's what she was trying to tell me. Complaining or whining will only make you sad and miserable and drag down everybody around you. If you want to be happy, think about happiness. If you want to have love, think, talk, and act with love.

There's a huge difference between living your life and letting your life be lived and deciding to live an intentional life is just like deciding to be happy or anything else you want to be. While it might not seem so simple if you feel trapped in a life that's the opposite of what you want, the choice is always yours. The first step is knowing how to build your intentions, and that's what you're going to learn in this chapter. Specifically:

- How to set the right intention, and how to identify when it *isn't* right
- How to own the impact we have on people and our environment
- How to be aware of the moments when we're boycotting our intentions and come back to the path we've chosen
- How to build an intentional life by establishing small intentions (creating missions)

Consider the story of James, a monk who was troubled by what he saw as a disturbance of the peace at the temple where he lived. Fellow monk John always had such terrible things to say about others and was a challenge for everybody who lived at the temple, but James was more troubled than the others. One day he went to his master about it.

"Master, I am tired of John's behavior," he said as he sat beside him on the bench in the garden of the monastery. "To excel in our meditation and evolve as a monk, we need peace, and John is taking it out of us."

"James, see that stone close to the river?" his master said. "Please go there and bring it to me."

Without understanding why his master wanted it, James went and picked up the stone. When James held it out to him, his master just smiled.

"James, are you able to give the stone to me?" he finally said.

"No," James said.

"But you are trying to give it to me, correct?"

"Yes."

"What will happen if I don't take it?"

"Well, I will keep it with me until I put it back in its place."

"Exactly. My intention is not to receive it, and what is yours?"

With a smile, the master turned to leave. But after taking a few steps, he looked back. "Know your intention and act according to it. Nobody can change it but you. You are ready to take my place when you learn how to do this."

If James wanted peace, he needed only to live in peace. The power of our intention is as strong as our thoughts about it. When something bothers us, it's not the thing itself that bothers us but our reaction to it, how we process the situation. James got stuck in his reaction to John's behavior, so in effect he sacrificed the peace he wanted for what he *didn't* want.

What if James refused to react to John's behavior? What if he just smiled like his master and refused what John was "offering" him?

If James were living his primary intention—his purpose—this is what would happen:

He identifies the annoyance he feels toward John and acknowledges it.

He takes a position as an observer of the situation and describes the feeling for himself. (When we make the effort to describe the emotion we have about a situation, we're labeling it, moving the processing of the experience from the limbic system to the prefrontal cortex.)

He returns to what he wants: living in peace to evolve as a monk (At this stage he's distanced himself from the emotions the situation had raised in him.)

He recognizes the situation as an opportunity to strengthen his skills of achieving what he wants and returning to equanimity

He models what he wants for John and others to see. In other words, he becomes the change he wants in the world.

If we live our primary intention and learn to live it integrally and coherently, wherever we are, whatever we're doing, our intention can happen exactly as we want. By having a clear intention in our mind, we can transform obstacles into challenges and challenges into opportunities. Lawyers, for example, use intentionality in their documents and contracts for the sake of clarity. When they create a legal document, they start with the "purpose of the document," the intention behind the writing, the reason the document exists, which serves as a guidepost for the rest of the document. If they find that they're deviating from the main purpose, they can go back and correct the document. More important, this guidance can help make the intention expressed in the purpose paragraph a reality. When anyone reads that first paragraph, they'll know how they can help to achieve the intention that's expressed.

If we write our own purpose paragraph clearly and explicitly, telling everyone around us what our intentions are, we can achieve the same success that results when legal contracts spell out the party's objectives. When others understand what we're trying to do, they'll step in to help us fulfill our life contract.

Our lives are guided by intention whether we realize it or not. Many of us don't wake up in the morning and think about our hopes for the day, and many of us don't even start the week writing or thinking about the priorities for the week. As a general rule, although there are those who make lists of New Year's resolutions, very few of us write about what we want for our lives, what kind of people we want to be, and what we'd like to leave behind. Obviously, we're underestimating the power of our intentions. And when we do that, we run the risk of getting caught in traps that jeopardize the beautiful journey our lives are supposed to be. And it's always harder to get ourselves out of the traps than it would have been to avoid them in the first place.

In my last assignment as a CEO, I was very happy that everything I've always asked for had been realized. I was in a country where I could make a difference, and I had a great leader who valued my human-focused style of leadership and a great team that was super enthusiastic about how we were building our business strategy. Our plan to completely transform the business had been in place for about three months, and it was getting better results than I could have hoped for. Among the many changes we made were a new bonus strategy based not on the number of bottles of medicine the sales team sold but on the number of lives they saved. We changed the language of the organization—for example, the Commercial Team became the Value Team—and adopted new strategic principles and a new operating model. The stakeholders were all in, and we became collaborators with our competitors in improving healthcare access, increasing the number of patients who could be treated instead of just competing to hold on to our respective market shares of the existing pie.

And then our global leadership announced a restructuring. We were assigned a new boss, and our regional boundaries were changed to encompass parts of Southeast Asia, Africa and eastern Europe. The people who'd approved and understood our strategy were no longer part of the company's leadership team. But the new boss was an old colleague whom I greatly admired, and I was optimistic about the changes. I wrote to him to share our plans and my ideas, and I told him I was happy that someone who believed in leading with clear vision was at the helm.

Over time, though, there were rumblings that the new boss intended to focus on the short term and realize more immediate results, and I started to fear that we'd be pressured to change our strategy and that my people and the stakeholders would be let down. Ultimately, I became motivated by fear instead of my intention to save patients, help the country, and prove that a corporation and its employees can work for good, and the boss's apparent aversion to my leadership style turned into a battle against our strategy. When I realized I was working out of fear, I tried to reverse the situation, explaining our strategy in even more detail in hopes that it would resonate with him, and I tried to connect with him through displays of respect, but by then it was too late. Our relationship had been damaged beyond repair.

My biggest lesson from the experience was that I *always* need to be aware of my intentions. My intentions had changed from trying to do something I believed in to trying to avoid something I was afraid of. Observe when your intentions are changing. Are you keeping what you want in mind or trying to avoid something? If you ask my leadership team what question I asked them the most in my first six months on the job, I'm sure they'd all remember it very clearly: "Okay, you've told me what you don't want—what do you *want*?" I only wish I'd asked myself that question as often as I asked them.

During my last ten years of leadership, I focused on what motivates human beings most. In reading about business, religion, and philosophy, I learned that helping people to live an intentional life makes the difference between having an organization that consists of ordinary people and having an organization that consists of people who are productive, efficient, and able to maintain balance in their lives. And it works for parenthood too. Being an intentional parent makes the difference between raising conscious children and raising children who only learn to follow the rules and will eventually make wrong choices because they think they can outsmart the system. Intentionality helps you make decisions that will make you a better person and ultimately give you the life you want.

The power of intention has been a basic tenet of many religions for centuries, with rules and commandments providing intentions designed to help people lead peaceful, fulfilled lives, but the connection between intention and spirituality goes beyond religious doctrine. Intentionality involves focusing our thoughts and actions toward a meaningful purpose, and by fostering intentional living we can cultivate a sense of connection to something larger than ourselves, regardless of specific religious beliefs. This concept presents a powerful tool for leaders. When leaders bring intentionality to their communities or workplaces, they contribute to a more spiritually connected world, fostering purpose and meaning beyond everyday tasks. And it all starts with knowing what you really want from your life.

Intentionality Unites Religions and Science

"The road to hell is paved with good intentions."
—Often attributed to Saint Bernard of Clairvaux

Religion's fundamental goal is to give people specific guidance for living a good life. All religions expect followers to live with the intention proposed by their line of thought in a manner that will represent a life well lived. In other words, religion's aim is to help find the right intention for living a fulfilled life.

Christianity teaches us to live according to God's will and use our intentions to serve others with love and compassion. Buddhism emphasizes living a mindful and compassionate life, focusing our intentions on freeing all beings from suffering. Similarly, Kabbalah guides us to live a life aligned with the divine light, making conscious choices that promote spiritual growth and avoid reactivity.

Even Eastern traditions like Hinduism, with its concept of *dharma* (righteous duty), guide us to live with intentionality, fulfilling our purpose in the universe according to our inherent nature. Taoism, emphasizing living in harmony with nature's flow, encourages us to make choices that consider the well-being of others, aligning intention with the natural order. Islam, emphasizing submission to God's will, teaches that living a life of good deeds requires deliberate and purposeful actions. Indigenous spiritualities around the world often focus on living in harmony with nature and community, which requires a deep sense of intention in one's actions and interactions.

Philosophers like Marcus Aurelius, Plato, and Zeno of Citium, the father of Stoicism, also talked about how to lead a fulfilled life. One way or another, all the major philosophers addressed the questions "What should I want in order to live a fulfilled life?" and "How do I make the right choices to get what I want?" Fundamental questions that have been on humans' minds forever.

By now, you might think we wouldn't need religion or philosophers to guide us to make the right decisions and be aware of our intentions. Unfortunately, while our culture and society teach us how to earn enough money to have a desirable lifestyle by developing marketable skills, we aren't taught how to be better people or understand our emotions and how they affect our lives. We don't learn to be aware that *everything* we do has either a positive or a negative impact on our lives and those of others. And that's where religion and philosophy come in. Although we're taught how to be intelligent, we have to learn how to be wise on our own unless we have a connection to a religion or a culture that values wisdom over intelligence.

I love the phrase I heard in my childhood more times than you can imagine: "Daughter, the road to hell is paved with good intentions." As I grew from adolescence to adulthood, I started to feel the weight of this wise saying. All actions will have a consequence, and while those actions might reflect your initial intention, they might also bring us the opposite of what we wanted. The way to achieve results that align with our initial intention is to develop our skills of discernment.

What exactly does that mean? Wikipedia defines discernment like this:

> ***Discernment** is the ability to obtain sharp perceptions or to judge well (or the activity of so doing). In the case of judgment, discernment can be psychological, moral or aesthetic in nature. Discernment has also been defined in the contexts; scientific (that is discerning what is true about the real world), normative (discerning value including what ought to be) and formal (deductive reasoning). The process of discernment within judgment involves going past the mere perception of something and making nuanced judgments about its properties or qualities. Discernment in the Christian religion is considered a virtue; a discerning individual is considered to possess wisdom and be of good judgment, especially with regard to subject matter often overlooked by others.*

As for the *process* of discernment, Wikipedia explains it like this:

> *The process of individual discernment has steps that can be taken in order to achieve a level of discernment. The following actions can be made when making decisions of discernment: taking time in making decisions, using both the head and heart, and assessing important values involved in the situation. Time has been considered necessary in the process of making a smart choice and decisions made in a hurry can be altered by lack of contemplation. When time is available to assess the situation, it improves the discernment process. When time allows, the tentative decision can be revisited days later and external people can be consulted to make sure that the individual is satisfied with their choice. Making decisions is involved with discernment and require both the "head" and the "heart." Making decisions with the "head" means to first reflect on the situation and emphasize the rational aspect of the decision-making process. In order to make a decision with the "heart," the individual needs to make decisions based on feelings as well as rationality. Values in the discernment process are weighing options that decide what is most important to the individual. Every individual's value system is different, which affects each individual*

discernment process. Combining values—using both the head and heart and taking sufficient time when making decisions—is the main step for a successful discernment process.

What I love about Wikipedia's explanation is that it calls out wisdom's role. Wisdom is a decision-making process based on the balance between our hearts and minds. We're wise when we can make decisions aligned with both our constructive intentions (which come from our mind) and our constructive emotions (which come from our heart), taking into account the impact they'll have on the integrality of our lives. We'll talk more about constructive emotions in Chapter 9, but for now suffice it to say that an intention to be constructive has to be based on a positive affirmation—yes to happiness instead of no to sadness—and motivated by a constructive emotion that involves compassion, such as love, or a higher purpose than anger, fear, or sadness.

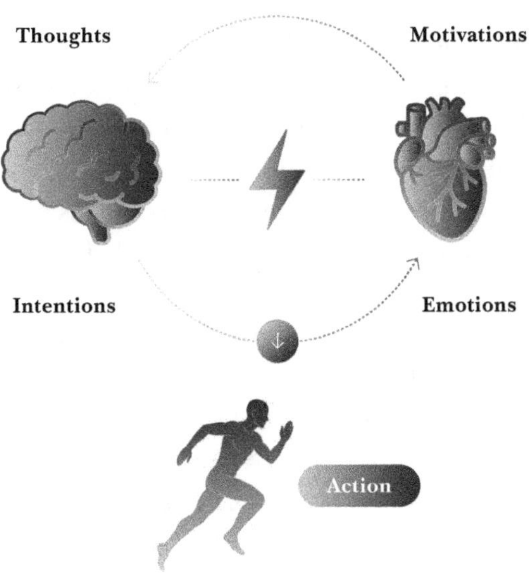

Figure 3

As depicted in the illustration above, the wrong emotions can affect our motivations by creating thoughts in opposition to our initial intentions. The outcome may be actions you hadn't intended. A person who's in love might take their love in the wrong direction when it's driven by fear of losing their loved one. Discernment means asking, *What do I really want?* Activating our frontal lobe by asking that logical question will align our hearts with our minds. We're applying reason to our emotions, thinking deeper about the decision we're making, and this prevents the wrong emotions from taking over. From a neuroscientific perspective, rationalizing emotions is a shift in brain activity from the amygdala, which triggers instinctive emotional responses, to the prefrontal cortex, which governs rational thought and decision-making. When we experience a strong emotion like anger or fear, the amygdala activates quickly, releasing stress chemicals and preparing the body for a reaction—often leading to impulsive decisions. However, when we take a step back and intentionally analyze our emotions, we engage the prefrontal cortex, allowing for cognitive reappraisal, emotional regulation, and more constructive decision-making. This process, which includes labeling emotions, reframing situations, and creating mental or physical distance, helps diminish the intensity of reactive emotions. Importantly, we don't "turn off" the amygdala but allow the prefrontal cortex to modulate its activity, ensuring that our responses align with both our logical reasoning and our deeper intentions. This ability to regulate emotions and bring coherence between heart and mind is essential for making thoughtful, purpose-driven decisions and maintaining emotional balance in leadership and life.

Just like emotions, intentions can be wrong in the sense that they can have a destructive effect. When we want something good for someone at a particular moment, we normally have good intentions, but if the emotion motivating us is fear, the resulting intention may be to prevent something negative from happening to the person. If what motivates your intention is destructive emotions, you're praying wrongly, so learn how to reframe it. Otherwise, the desire to avoid something will only focus your energy and thoughts on what can go wrong, and that could prove to be a self-fulfilling prophecy.

Wisdom is cultivated through the conscious development of intentionality, allowing us to shape our spiritual growth beyond religious or philosophical frameworks. It emerges when we refine our ability to discern, align, and act—choosing responses that arise from constructive intentions and motivations rather than reactive impulses. By strengthening our capacity to make decisions that honor both our inner truth and the systems we engage with, we create coherence in our lives, living intentionally and purposefully in every action we take.

Some scientists believe that everything that happens to us is the result of our genetics, that we don't have any influence on our biology or our lives. They believe that most diseases, including diabetes and cancer, come from our genes and that our parents' genetic heritage will define our temperament, personality, and psychological traits. But developmental biologist Bruce Lipton, author of *The Biology of Belief*, says it's our perceptions of life that shape our biology. Based on his research of epigenetics—the science that investigates how the environment and our life experiences select, modify, and regulate gene activity—he says that our brain cells secrete chemicals in response to the way the brain interprets what's happening around us and that these chemicals dictate our behavior and our biology. (This is a highly simplified explanation of the complex process.)

In his book, he makes his intention very clear:

> *The intention behind this book is to translate the significance of this leading-edge science so that it is accessible to the lay audience. It is my sincerest hope that you will recognize that many of the beliefs propelling your life are false and self-limiting and you will be inspired to change these beliefs. Understanding on a scientific level how cells respond to your thoughts and perceptions illuminates the path to personal empowerment. The insights we gain through this new biology unleash the power of consciousness, matter and miracles.*

And over the course of the book, Lipton fulfills his intention. He shows us the power we all have to define our lives and biology by the way we see life and ourselves. He demonstrates the importance of revisiting our beliefs and creating new ones to align with our intentions. In other words, he confirms the importance of living an intentional life, setting clear intentions and living beliefs that will help us create the future and the world we want to live in.

While this may sound more like a philosophy or a religion than a science, it's actually spirituality. Scientists who study life to this degree often come to spiritual conclusions and, in the process, become wise guides who can help us along the path of our lives. Two of my favorite quotes about how thoughts and perceptions guide our lives come from scientists:

"The most important decision we make is whether believe we live in a friendly or a hostile universe." – Albert Einstein

"Change the way you look at things, and things you look at will change." – Maxwell Planck

But advice is cheap, right? What about the "how"? Once we understand how critical intentionality is, how can we *live* it? How can we use it to spiritually transform ourselves into what we want to be and someone we'll be proud of?

Good questions. Read on.

Intentionality Can Be a Way of Life

Intentionality has been an important part of my life for decades, ever since I figured out that when my mother used to say, "Do you want to be happy? Then be it!" she was teaching me how to ask for things. She said that if we want peace, we need to say, "We want peace," because if we simply say no to war, we're putting our focus on the war and it won't necessarily bring peace.

In my professional life, I've used intentionality by always having a clearly defined vision, mission, and purpose as the basis for strategies

I work with. I've done the same in my private life, but my purpose is always evolving, and as it does, the visions I create for my missions evolve along with them.

Since an early age, my purpose has been to be happy. At first my vision of what *happy* meant consisted of moments of happiness, and I executed small missions in various areas of my life to achieve that vision, such as investing time in yoga, swimming, and having good friends. As I got older and my leadership responsibilities grew, being happy became much more complex. Being happy didn't depend only on myself anymore. I couldn't be happy if the people around me weren't happy or if I hadn't at least done my best to build environments where they had a chance to be happy. During my first years in higher leadership positions, I suppressed an important potential inside me out of the belief that personal happiness was a selfish goal. My new purpose was to make the people around me happy. I studied Kabbalah and the *Yoga Sutras.* I read about Bhutan and its government-instituted Gross National Happiness Index, with its emphasis on aspects of well-being that aren't related to money. I read about Zappos, the online shoe retailer that makes an art of customer service and enjoys off-the-charts repeat business. In each area of my life, I was building visions that would help us all to get what we wanted by exploring our purposes and aligning our lives' goals.

Then more systems were added to my life when we were blessed with the arrival of our kids. We couldn't baptize them until the adoption was finalized and the kids' names were legally changed in four to five years, but we wanted to start bringing some spirituality to their lives. To take them to the church would have been a challenge because there would be pressure to baptize them without their definitive names, so instead we found a great ten-week course, "Spirituality for Kids: Winning the Game of Life," and every Sunday we spent three hours working on the program at a Kabbalah center. One of my own biggest takeaways from the course was the idea that all of us are light. We're all here to illuminate the path we deserve in life as well as others' paths. Whenever we experience difficult situations, it's because something is blocking our light. Darkness doesn't exist—it's merely the absence of light, and without light, we develop negative motivations and make poor decisions. If kids choose to play video games instead of doing homework, it's motivated by the desire for short-term compensation—instant happiness. They're not considering the consequences of that decision. It's as if a blanket is blocking the light.

Fortunately, making good decisions is as easy as moving the blanket out of the way. When your path is illuminated, you'll probably choose to do your homework and earn yourself more time to play on weekends, and this "work ethic" will benefit your life as a whole. It's the difference between true plenitude and instant happiness.

Suddenly, thanks to this program for kids, I understood where I was going wrong. Instead of trying to make others happy, let alone myself, I should be pursuing true plenitude, starting with having peace inside myself.

Aha!

Our inner peace and fulfillment are more important than short-term happiness, and they depend on how capable we are of seeing the integrality of situations and helping others to see it too. This change in my perspective also brought a change in my purpose. With absolute clarity about it, I put it in writing: *To be at peace by helping others find their purpose in life and living a life that makes the world a better place for everyone.*

Five Insights Toward Plenitude and Light

Everyone is light. There might be moments of darkness because of decisions that block the light. This prevents people from being fully happy.

To live fulfilled and in peace, you must learn the difference between instant happiness and true plenitude.

True plenitude has everything to do with knowing how to turn on your own light by making the right decisions, keeping in mind the systems you're in (your life and others' lives).

When you consider the systems around you, with you included, you're connecting your long-term happiness (true plenitude) with the impact you have on others. So knowing your life's meaning (purpose) is directly proportional to your happiness.

Bringing light to anyone's life requires living with discernment, being aware of the beliefs that guide life, and being 100 percent clear about what you want in life.

And then another insight came to me: We all have what it takes to live in plenitude because we're all light, unless there's a blanket hiding the light. And what brings the blanket to our lives is the filters that guide you to wrong decisions. People are misled by destructive decisions, but in essence we're all good.

I also had absolute clarity that I believe in all human beings and love all human beings. I might not like some of their decisions and might not agree with some of their choices, but I love them because everyone has potential that just needs to be turned on. As a result, I assigned myself a new mission: to find that potential in others. At work, I'd unleash the potential of my people to bring value to their lives. At home, I'd believe in my husband and kids so they could believe in themselves and do their best. In my community and with my friends, I'd help them collaborate with each other to unleash our collective potential.

And that's what I've done. Wherever I am, I help others create visions of what we'd like to see happen in our lives so we can align our individual purposes to a common view. I help bring intentionality to their lives.

Skills for Living an Intentional Life

Let's look at four important skills we can all develop to live the intentional life: *self-awareness, building our personality constructively, identifying emotional motivations, and reframing.* These skills will help you build the path to living a life motivated by the right emotions and identify when you've strayed from the path and come back to it.

With Self-awareness, We Can Continually Build Personality

As we know by now, our decisions and how we live, consciously or unconsciously, will determine our personality and who we are as human beings. As much as we try to build an image or live up to the expectations of our different environments (work, family, friends), what we are Iwill always come to the surface. Unless we're conscious about who we are and what we want and we can live by it in all our environments, we'll lead stressful lives and suffer terrible identity crises. The best leaders, parents, and friends are the ones who inspire us because of their coherent way of living. Disappointment comes when we see a lack of coherence. Ever hear the saying "Never meet your heroes"? That's why. On the other hand, we can also admire someone when we know their vulnerabilities if those vulnerabilities indicate how they're growing and learning from their mistakes and moving toward where they want to go.

An easy way to start to live an intentional life is by simply deciding how we want to live and understanding how decisions lead to action. This style of leadership will allow you to explain your decision-making process, making it easier for people to understand you and your actions. What are the assumptions behind the decisions you make? And what are the emotions and beliefs behind your assumptions? Behind all our decisions is a set of beliefs that ground our thoughts. Our beliefs can include hidden biases that interfere with our clarity about how we make decisions, and that's our worst enemy in the journey to becoming the person we want to be.

Identifying the emotions that create the biases behind our assumptions allows us to better understand our decision-making process, and *that* gives us the tool we need to make the changes necessary to become who we want to be. Without that tool, we can't take the huge step toward becoming more conscious and enhancing our self-awareness.

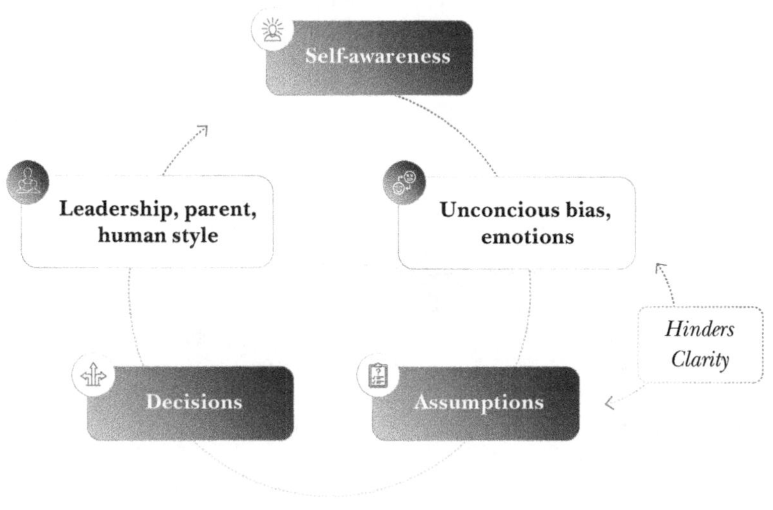

Figure 4

Our emotions can have a strong effect on our decisions because they can trigger memories with powerful positive or negative associations. When we're tired, sick, or experiencing other physical difficulty, our brain is likely to associate the situation with negative memories. In better moments, moments of peace, our brain is likely to make positive associations. And the more often our brain makes these associations, the higher the probability that it will return to these memories, because the neuronal connections being made serve as a filter for finding *similar* memories.

Fortunately, we're not at the mercy of associations run amok. There's a way to choose what neural connections to build, what kind of filter we want our brains to use. It's a process called *neuroplasticity*—replacing old neural connections with new ones— and we can use it to guide our brains to make the right decisions. It's a question of habit. A learning habit.

Depending on the memory our brain finds, it will trigger an emotion that's positive or negative, and the thoughts that follow will reflect those emotions. In the case of extreme emotions like love and rage, we'll react to the situation with an action that might represent only our heart, meaning the emotion is speaking and acting for us. But if we can understand the memory and the emotion it causes, we can choose how to act. Instead of reacting to the moment, we'll act consciously, considering our true intentions, and make decisions with our hearts and minds aligned.

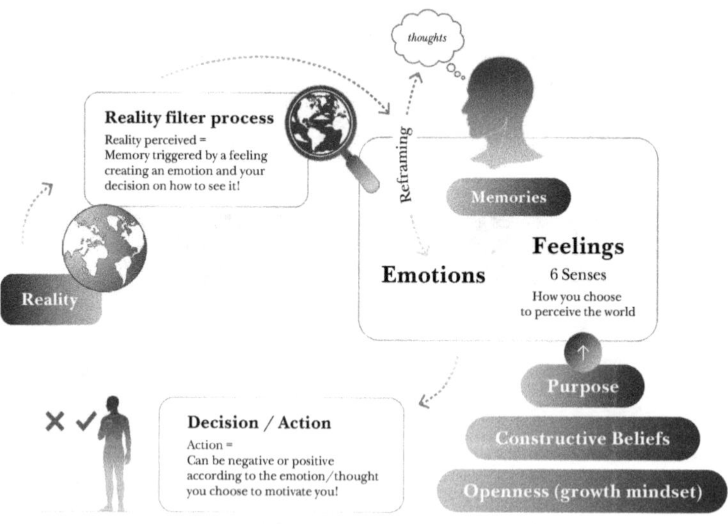

Figure 5

There's a Cherokee proverb where an elder of the tribe offers his grandson some guidance about life. "Every day, a fight is going on inside us," he says. "It is the most important fight for us. It is between two wolves. One is evil—he has anger, envy, sorrow, regret, greed, arrogance, self-pity, guilt, resentment, inferiority, lies, false pride, superiority, and ego. The other is good—he is joy, peace, love, hope, serenity, humility, kindness, benevolence, empathy, generosity, truth, compassion, and faith."

The grandson thinks about it for a moment. "Which wolf will win?" he finally asks.

His grandfather smiles. "The one you feed."

The wolf we feed is the neural connections we build. This is the power of neuroplasticity. We can induce our brains to automatically create neuronal connections that allow us to enhance our cognitive maturity, our power to make better decisions. And if we have this awareness, we're likely to start paying more attention to the thoughts we allow ourselves to have. By living with a clear purpose, clear beliefs and a growth mindset—open to learning from everything that happens in our lives— we can wire our brains positively. And this will feed the cycle of good feelings, thoughts, and actions.

Now let's look at how to do it.

We Can Build Our Personality by Focusing on What We Want

Given that our decisions build our personalities and that our thoughts and emotions affect our decisions, the key to building the personality we want and living a life that positively impacts others is knowing what we want and choosing the thoughts and emotions that support that outcome. And in determining what we want, we establish our purpose. To live a life that will have a more positive impact on others, we need to take three steps:

- Determine what we want in life
- Identify moments when we aren't living in clarity and bring ourselves back on track
- Reframe our thoughts to bring them back to what we want instead of what we want to avoid

Many of us believe that purpose is for heroes or people who spend lots of time looking within, but purpose is built on a series of simple questions we can all ask ourselves:

- What kind of person do I want to be?
- What would I like to be remembered for?
- What is it that I can help others with?
- Why do I do what I do?
- Why don't I do what I don't do?

When you live an intentional life, your purpose emerges naturally, and you'll eventually *pursue* it naturally. At first it might seem that your actions stem from selfishness rather than a desire to help others, but that's actually a component of purpose. In *Purposehood: Transform Your Life, Transform the World*, Ammar Charani says our purpose is meant to be both altruistic and selfish. Doing good for the world around us benefits us as well, and that should be part of our motivation. According to Charani's "Purposehood of Everything Theory," everything has a purpose, and finding ours allows us to align with the universe and live with ease and plenitude.

What we believe in is also very important to building the wisdom needed for a life of plenitude. Our beliefs will become truths that guide our lives. This awareness is the difference between success and failure in making a change in our personality. We all have unconscious bias—truths and beliefs we aren't aware of—and they're the biggest threat to our success, so the more we can become aware of them, the more successful we'll be.

Exercise 3 – Limiting or Abundant Beliefs? What Am I Feeding My Life With?

Make a list of the most important beliefs you want to have in life—and follow it.

Starting reflection: Your beliefs will be the foundation of the human being you want to be. You have to be clear about what they are and be able to communicate them clearly to others. This is the only way to live a coherent and consistent life.

Reflect on the stories you tell about your past and future—the stories you tell about your childhood, your relationships, your parents, etc.—and then ask yourself:

- What do I strongly fight for?
- What do I strongly fight against?
- What do I need to have in my life?
- What could I never cope with?

Guiding questionnaire: Your thoughts form your beliefs, which become the truths that positively or negatively guide your decision-making process. By reflecting on the impact your thoughts have on your legacy, you can take the first step toward reframing your way of making decisions. The following exercise will guide your reflections:

Answer each question in the answer column.

Considering the legacy you want to leave, your purpose, and the person you want to be remembered as, write "+1" if the belief you've written is in alignment with those goals and your purpose, and write "-1" if the belief is in conflict with them (or neutral).

	QUESTION	ANSWER	+1/-1 impact on decisions
Core Values	What are the most important principles that guide your life? (e.g., honesty, compassion, fairness)		
	When faced with a difficult decision, which principles do you prioritize?		
	How do your actions reflect your stated values?		
Purpose and Meaning	What gives your life meaning and purpose? What motivates you to get out of bed in the morning?		
	What kind of impact do you want to make on the world?		
	How do your daily actions contribute to your overall purpose?		
Self-awareness	What are your strengths and weaknesses? How do they influence your decisions?		
	What are your deepest fears and desires?		
	How do your emotions affect your judgment?		
Relationships and Community	How do you define a good and healthy relationship?		
	What kind of legacy do you want to leave for the people you care about?		
	What role do you want to play in your community?		
Worldview and Morality	What ethical principles guide your actions?		
	How do you approach complex social issues?		
	What is your responsibility to the environment and future generations?		
Growth and Learning	How important is continuous learning and self-improvement to you?		
	What are you willing to do to challenge your own assumptions and biases?		
	How do you handle mistakes and setbacks?		
Spirituality	Do you believe in a higher power or spiritual dimension?		
	How does your spirituality, if any, inform your values and actions?		
	What practices or rituals help you connect with your inner self?		

Concluding reflection:

Look back at each answer that received a -1 and reflect on these questions:

- Is this belief based on fear, social conditioning, or past pain?
- What belief would better align with my values and desired impact?
- What new narrative can I write for myself based on clarity, not reaction?

Below you can check your score and evaluate if your decision-making process is positively or negatively affected by how you're living your life. Being honest with the answers will allow you to identify the areas of life where a shift in perspective could have a strong positive effect on your decisions and, in turn, the results you see from your actions.

0–7 points: Your inner compass needs recalibration

Your responses suggest that many of your current beliefs may not be serving the future you desire or the legacy you want to leave. Some may be inherited, shaped by fear, or simply outdated. This result isn't a failure; it's a powerful opportunity to take back authorship of your story. This is your invitation to begin reshaping your framework of truth—to lead a life that feels like yours. Now is the moment to reframe your beliefs according to what you need and want from your life.

8–14 points: You're in the process of alignment

You're walking the path of coherence. Some beliefs are already aligned with your values and purpose, while others may still reflect unresolved fears, unconscious patterns, or moments when you felt you had no other option. This is a transition space, rich with potential.

Look especially at patterns in your **Self-Awareness**, **Worldview**, and **Purpose** sections. These areas often hold clues about your unconscious drivers. Reflect on these questions:

- Which beliefs energize and ground me?
- Where do I still feel tension or contradiction?
- How can I better integrate constructive emotions into my decision-making?

This is a time for refinement. The more intentional you become, the clearer your path will be. Be conscious about your beliefs and where they're leading you. Grow your discernment and remember that everything has consequences.

15–21 points: You're living at a high level of coherence

Your beliefs are well-aligned with your purpose, values, and the legacy you want to leave. You've built a solid inner compass that allows you to make decisions with clarity, confidence, and compassion. You aren't perfect—none of us are—but your intentionality is visible in how you show up in the world.

Your answers across sections—especially in **Core Values, Relationships and Community**, and **Spirituality**—probably reveal that your beliefs uplift both your life and the systems you belong to. Keep revisiting and refining your beliefs as you evolve. Stay curious and open to learning from others without losing your center. And use your coherence to inspire and elevate those around you.

Keep in mind the beliefs you're nurturing and how they're building who you're becoming. Beware of any new beliefs and seize the moment to reevaluate where you want to go. It's essential to be aware of the impact you have on those around you. Remember, we're all leaders, and at any moment we're affecting others with our unconscious beliefs. Reframe or reinforce those beliefs to serve your purpose.

**

When you're conscious of your beliefs and you implement them in your life, you're nurturing your discernment. Every decision in your life has consequence, and when you use discernment correctly, you'll be handsomely rewarded. Take the example of a teacher's simple decision about how to respond when students are being disrespectful. In Switzerland, society is built on respect, and some schools employ an interesting method of getting children to listen to the teacher: When the classroom is filled with noisy chatter while the teacher is speaking, the teacher speaks more and more softly until the students who *are* paying attention ask the others to stop talking. The teacher only returns to a normal voice when everyone is silent. This is a very coherent response. Intentionally, the teacher respects the children by not raising his or her voice and allows the children who want to listen to lead. In the end, the teacher is rewarded with the children's respect without having to shout or disrespect *them.*

When we have a purpose, whether it's to cultivate a respectful society or inner peace or happiness, we can see the big picture of possibilities for achieving it. When my father asked me whether I wanted to be pregnant or be a mother while I was undergoing in vitro treatment, he forced me to ask myself what I really wanted and I was able to face the situation clearly. I realized that families can start from diverse situations, and I let go of the desire to become pregnant. I realized that I just wanted a family and that I could achieve that another way. Knowing when to ask ourselves what we really want can save us from making many bad decisions in the course of our lives. Sometimes we're so focused on problems that we have a hard time seeing even obvious solutions, but being intentional in our daily lives wires our brains in a way that allows us to see them more easily.

Identifying Our Emotional Motivators Enhances Clarity

During one of my yearly strategy reviews while I was working in India and Venezuela, I led my team of directors in an exercise where we identified where in our bodies certain emotions were felt. There's an emotion behind anything we do, and for reference we used the scale of motivations in the book *Quantum Leader*, by Professor Danah Zohar, one of my greatest inspirations in life. Zohar's husband, psychoanalyst Ian Marshall, built the scale based on more than twenty years of experience in his clinic.

Unlike famous American psychologist Abraham Maslow, who believed that all of human behavior is dictated by five needs, Marshall believed that what motivates people is their emotions. A person experiencing fear will act in a destructive manner even when all five levels of need in "Maslow's Hierarchy" are fulfilled. And a person experiencing positive emotions will act in a constructive manner even when none of their basic needs are being met.

The stories about people living in concentration camps that Viktor Frankl shares in *Man's Search for Meaning* are an indication that Marshall is correct. Frankl, a psychiatrist and neurologist at the University of Vienna Medical School, spent his life researching and writing about the impact of a life guided by purpose and the difference that having a purpose made in the lives of people enduring hardships.

Marshall's motivation scale has eight negative and eight positive motivations, and each of the eight negatives has a positive that can offset it (see the graph below). When our team of directors studied the scale, we learned how to identify when the negative emotions were appearing, and then we worked on how to reframe them. We started to use the scale in both countries, and then we cascaded it down to the organization, which gave us all a common language for talking about our emotions in a scientific manner.

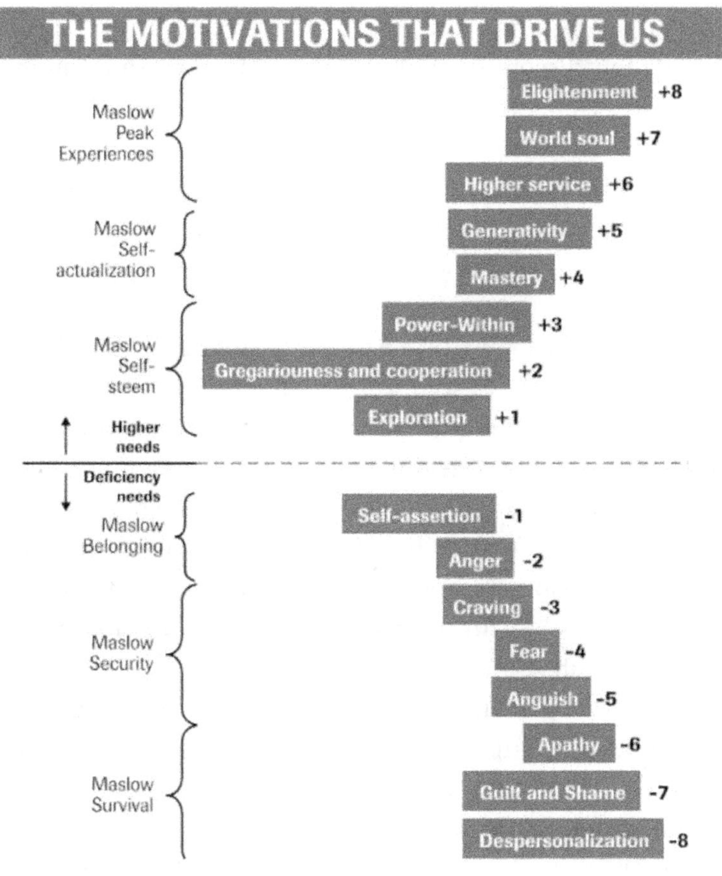

Figure 6

Reframing Is an Intentional Superpower

If we can identify when a certain destructive emotion is arising, we can "park" the emotion (acknowledge it and put it aside for a while) and reframe it, making sure the action that follows it won't be destructive but rather taken intentionally, employing discernment and awareness of the consequences of decisions and actions guided by the wrong emotion. Easier said than done, right? Not really.

In the same training session with the directors, we learned that whenever we felt discomfort, it was a sign that something unexpected was happening. Depending on how our brains are wired or the mood we're in at the moment, discomfort can unleash a sequence of negative thoughts that lead to a negative course of action. But what if every time we feel discomfort, we remember what we really want and focus our thoughts on it? This would lead instead to a chain of thoughts "lightened" by the possibility of getting what we want.

This is how we can use intentionality to frame any situation so that we see with clarity despite our emotional clouds. The key is to create the habit of asking ourselves what we want after observing the discomfort that arises in our bodies and identifying whether the thoughts we have are actually about avoidance of what we *don't* want. When our behavior is focused on what we want—on purpose, missions and visions—we inspire others and lead them toward framing decision-making processes with positive thoughts and opening the door to abundance while shutting out limiting thoughts.

A situation, an environment, or a person can spark emotions that blur your mind, robbing you of clarity, and decisions made at these times usually have negative consequences. That's where intentionality comes in. If we have a purpose and are clear on what we want in life, these moments won't last long enough to harm us. Eventually, we'll develop the habit of returning to what we really want instead of letting what we don't want control our emotions and our decision-making. Maybe if I'd made it a habit by the time I was assigned a new boss, I wouldn't have responded from a place of fear. Maybe I would have lived what I believed and enjoyed the positive outcome of our strategy.

On the other hand, unfamiliar emotions that bring fear might indicate that something new and beautiful is emerging. There are five steps we can take to reframe unfavorable situations so we can see what's emerging—the opportunities within the unexpected:

LEADING SITUATIONS

How to see the emerging future?

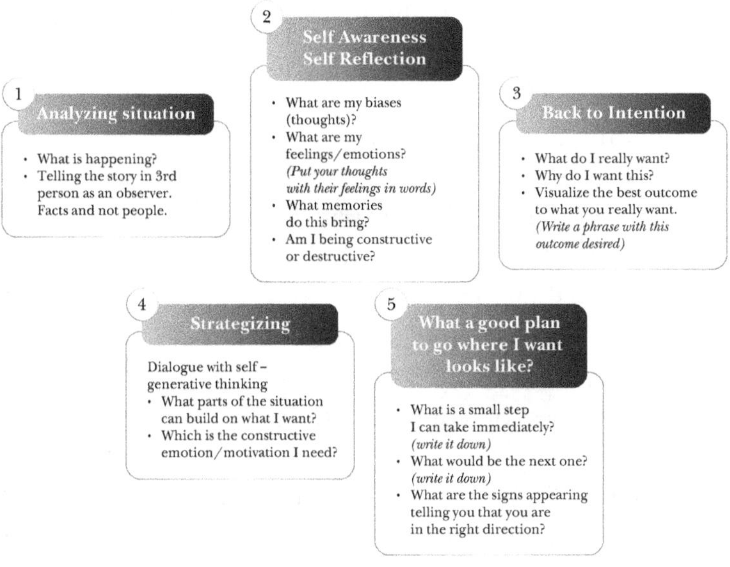

Figure 7

Analyze the situation

Step back from the situation and describe the facts of the situation. Refrain from talking about people or expressing opinions about what's happening.

In your head or on paper (or on your computer screen), compose an objective report of what's happening. Rather than using first person ("I"), use third person (your name and "he/she"). And stick to the facts: "When X happened, (your name here) did Y."

Reflect on your self-awareness

Also in third person, list the thoughts that are coming to your mind, with all the nuances and shades of gray, but without judging. Answer the questions:

- What are my thoughts?
- What are the emotions I feel right after these thoughts?
- What memories do these thoughts and feelings bring?
- Are these thoughts, feelings and memories constructive or destructive?

Return to the intention

- Ask yourself: What do I really want?
- Ask yourself: Why do I want this? (Here you'll start to identify what's motivating you. If your answer is "to avoid X," or "not to have X," or any other negative, go back and ask again until the answer is a positive.)
- Visualize the best outcome of getting what you want.

Ask the following questions in a conversation with yourself. After you answer, say "And ..." and open yourself to any constructive thoughts that may come. If they don't come, say, "And what more can we think of?"

- What parts of this situation can I build on to get what I want in the future?
- What is the constructive emotion I need?
- What is my purpose in life and how I can live it in this situation?

Create a plan for getting where you want to go

- Write down a first small step you can take now.
- Write down the next step.
- Identify signs that indicate you're moving in the right direction.
- Identify people around you who can benefit from this situation together with you.
- Write down how these people will benefit and talk to them about it.

This exercise changed my life more than once. Forcing myself to focus on what I wanted and asking myself the right questions has opened my field of abundance. The moment my new boss at Roche informed me that he was releasing me from my position as Roche Pharma India CEO and directed me not to look for a different position in the company, all my fears were realized. I was going to lose the biggest opportunity I'd ever had to work in a coherent way: to do good while realizing great results and to focus on people and the country and inspire my team and everyone around me to do the same. I was going to lose the opportunity to show everyone that we can love our jobs and have a safe space at work where we even talk about our fears. I was going to lose the opportunity to create a better working life for others. I went home to discuss the situation with my husband before letting HR know whether I'd be accepting their offer. And that's when I had my revelation: *This is the biggest opportunity yet for me to live what I believe. I'll act in gratitude to everyone who's involved in this moment and reflect on what I really want.* Maybe this was an opportunity to help on a scale bigger than my team and even my company and discover what I was really here for.

At that moment, I was clear that I'd never choose to leave Roche. I loved what I was doing, I loved my team, and I loved the company. I just didn't get along with my boss. Ultimately, I told him he'd need to fire me because I wasn't willing to create the appearance that I didn't believe in what my team had worked so hard for. Life was clearly telling me I should start a company that would spread my beliefs to leaders and anyone else who wanted to build a better world where working would be a gift and a blessing, not an obligation.

By doing the above exercise and fueling myself with certainty that this would be the best decision for me, I was able to make the decision with love in my heart, even for my boss. In the end, I reframed one of the most difficult moments of my life into a great learning experience and built a memory that wasn't harmful but was instead framed by gratitude.

Purpose Is Fundamental for Intentionality

Having a clear purpose is the most important step we have to take to live an intentional life. Just like the "purpose of the document" spells out the intention behind a legal document and keeps the author focused as he writes, having a purpose will define who we are and guide us in the right direction throughout our lives. This clarity will allow us to know exactly when we need to review our purpose and reanalyze our lives. And the younger we are when we start living a life with purpose, the faster we'll learn to identify when we have to switch gears.

As our lives evolve and encompass more and more people, environments, and systems, our purpose might shift direction from time to time. Our reason for living may change when we become parents, for example. Being aware of this is essential to flowing with life rather than struggling through each transformation we face. Life is change, and while change can bring struggle, it can also bring growth. Having a purpose that changes with our lives makes the ride much more enjoyable, allowing us to always live coherently and have a positive impact on others.

When you start living coherently—when you're the same person in all areas of your life— your purpose will become a natural part of whatever you do. Others will help you, and even when they aren't with you, they'll be thinking about how they can help you. You'll notice that circumstances are aligning with what you want in life. Actually, they've always been aligning with your goals—you just didn't notice because you weren't focused on what really matters.

There's nothing like the feeling that the universe is conspiring with us. Others always seem to be helping us, and there's a sense of synchronicity about everything that happens. Even when something painful happens, we ultimately realize that it was necessary for keeping us on the right path—what appear to be detours actually take us closer to what we want. That's what happens when our lives are in alignment with our purpose, and in the next chapter we'll learn the art of bringing it all together.

CHAPTER 7

OUR PURPOSE CAN INSPIRE OUR MISSIONS

"What is essential is invisible to the eye, but deeply felt by the heart."
—Antoine de Saint-Exupéry

When I was living in Venezuela as president of Roche, my routine was challenging—meetings with various chambers of commerce where I was a board member, negotiating with the government to bring medicine into the country, endless talks with the team to mitigate out-of-stock scenarios, the constant fear that the company would have to leave the country. And still I arrived home to be mother to my kids—sharing homework-helper duties with my husband, listening to their problems at school and discussing possible solutions, having dinner together most nights. Even with my head full of professional concerns, I took part in whole-family meditations and gratitude rounds where we shared the day's happenings that we were grateful for before putting the kids to bed. One night right after we'd gotten into bed, I was telling my husband I was worried about the situation in the country but also impressed with the team's response to my strategy to be transparent and work for something bigger than our salaries, namely our country and the patients using our medicines. He suddenly stopped me.

"I'm not sure why, but ever since I've known you, you've been consistent about everything you say and do," he said. "What you preach at work, you do at home. What you keep saying at home, I see you doing at work. For all these years I've watched you following a clear path without deviating from it." Even though it was dark, I could see that he looked a little mystified. "Even when things get tough, you always find a way to get through it with the same spirit, living what you believe."

I thought about it for a while. "I think it's because I know what I want in life," I finally said. "Since long ago. And I always come back to it."

That's when I started to realize just how important it is to follow our purpose. The determination to be a good human had always guided my decisions, and I could see that ever since I came to understand my purpose, decisions had become less and less complicated. Being the same person as a president of a company, as a mother, as a sister, as a wife, as a daughter, and as a friend made life easier. I have difficult moments and challenging situations, but even when I make a mistake, I know where I want to go as a human being, which makes it easier to correct my course of action. This is also one of the reasons why I was able to climb the multinational corporate ladder while also having a rewarding private life—consistency, my coherence in life.

I had clear missions in regard to my children, my company, my husband, my friends, my family, and the boards I was part of. I wanted to bring spirituality to the world, a belief that we can live for something more than ourselves.

In the organizations I worked for, my mission was to make my people happy by working with them toward their purpose and encouraging them to think about how they could benefit society through their work.

In the chambers and associations I was part of, I always strongly advocated a decision-making process where we would collaborate with governments and stakeholders in the best interests of society, not just our own interests.

In my family, I encouraged awareness of our decisions and the impact we made in the world, always with the greater good in mind.

I had a mission for every environment of my life and I communicated it. This made it easier to live my purpose and my intentions simply because it cleared the way for others to help me. Because they knew exactly what I wanted, they knew exactly what they could do to help me fulfill my purpose, which in turn fulfilled *them.*

Coherence is about being vocal, vulnerable, and consistent. It's about aligning your communication, behavior, and missions in life, and inspiring others in the process. Knowing how to tell your story in each area of your life based on your purpose allows you to live your life authentically, free of the need for masks or any other pretenses. It allows you to live life in its totality and integrality. Living in coherence is like the wind—you can't see it, but you can feel it. And so can everyone it inspires.

Being Coherent Means Framing Your Life with Your Purpose

In the first four years after leaving the corporate world, I mentored more than four hundred executives from multinationals around the world. One of my challenges was to help each of them find their purpose, and the progress reports they continue to give me about how their professional and private lives have evolved since then indicate that our sessions were successful and motivate me to keep at it.

Here's a sampling of what they've told me:

"I'm able to be myself at work for the first time. Since I feel this way, my work is much better, and my productivity has increased!"

"Since we're doing purpose exercises at work, I have changed how I see my private and professional life. Work became part of my life and not an obligation."

"Living my purpose at work makes me proud of doing what I do, and I can talk about my dreams as they align with my professional goals!"

"I never thought I would teach coworkers to live their purpose and deal better with their emotions. This is much more aligned with my purpose in life. I love my work."

"For many years, I didn't tell my family what I used to do at work. I wanted to keep my professional and private life separated. But for the last few months, I've been coming home and telling my daughter what I'm doing, and she is so proud of me. Things have changed at home since this."

"Leading a team that works for its purpose is much easier. Mistakes are communicated faster, risks are taken more consciously, and we can be better leaders because people don't shy away from expressing what they want because they trust you more easily. This is so different, so much better."

"Because of finding my purpose, I decided to leave the company. It is scary, but I knew I would never be my best version there. However, I know what I want in life, and I am pursuing it."

The difference between living with purpose and without purpose becomes especially evident in the decision-making that occurs during crises and other situations where risk-taking is necessary. At our most important moments in life, when absolutely nothing is predictable and we're afraid of uncertain circumstances and outcomes, we tend to obsess over everything that can go wrong and make plans to avoid it. But *that's* what makes things go wrong. Otto Scharmer, author of *Theory U: Leading from the Emerging Future: From Ego-System to Eco-System Economies,* says that wherever our thoughts go, our energy follows, and whatever we devote our energy to, that's what we manifest in our lives. So if you focus your thoughts on what can go wrong, it *will* go wrong.

In business, we often make the same mistake. We create a "mitigation plan" that lists potential solutions for everything that could go wrong with a strategy and assign a person to monitor the situation—to look for trouble. But we should also list the potential outcomes of realizing our purpose. I saw many plans go wrong as leaders focused their plans entirely on mitigation. They prepared a launch and knew what they wanted to achieve and how they wanted their product to enter the market and make a difference in their clients' lives... but then came the analysis of their competitors. It made them so nervous that they changed their whole strategy to focus on beating the competition by showing their competitors' weakness and faults instead of focusing on what their new product could really bring to their clients. All this did was create confusion about the product itself, regardless of the manufacturer, and nobody won. It cast doubt on *every* company's product, including their own, and sales suffered for all of us.

Companies need to remember why they're selling the products they're selling. Talking about a competitor, even if it's to point out how superior your company is, only serves to draw attention to the competitor and away from *your* product, and that's not the stuff of great product launches. We used to tell our salespeople, "If you have only one shot with the doctor, focus on talking about our products and why they're so good for the patients, what we want to offer to them. Focus on *what we want to sell.* Don't talk about the competitor. Otherwise, that's what will be stuck in our doctors' minds." Sure, they might have persuaded doctors not to buy from the competition, but they also would have squandered the opportunity to sell *our* product because they didn't spend any time talking about its benefits. The result: The doctors will give their business to a salesperson who does talk about the benefits of what they're selling.

When we have a few moments to think about our decisions, we should focus on what we want. Otherwise, what we *don't* want will be stuck in our minds. In the end, we might avoid what we don't want, but we surely won't get what we do want. When we're aware of the stories we're telling ourselves, it becomes easier to foresee their outcomes. If the stories are driven by fear, rage, or sadness, we can foresee that in trying to avoid something, we'll be stuck in the cycle of fear and avoidance, incapable of seeing the situation and any opportunities that may be present with clarity. And then we have to figure out how to bring our focus back to what we *want.* But if we live based on our purpose and values, it takes much less time and effort to redirect our focus when facing difficult decisions or situations.

People living their purpose are the creators of their lives, while those who choose to avoid specific outcomes are victims of adverse circumstances. At some point in their lives, they're going to ask themselves, *How did I get here?* It's all about telling the right stories, stories about your purpose. As we'll see in the next section, knowing your purpose will help the universe to conspire with you.

In the figures below you can see summaries of a life lived with purpose and a life lived without purpose. Most lives lived without purpose are passive, marked by decisions that might take us to surprising destinies, many not positive. And any of the destinies will be consequences of unplanned circumstances, where you're unconscious of the decisions that brought you to where you are.

When you live an intentional life, where your purpose guides your most difficult decisions and biggest challenges, your final destiny might be different from what you planned, but it will be much better than you expected. In each step of a life driven by purpose, infinite possibilities are presented and a life of abundant possibilities is unleashed, demonstrated by the many people and circumstances that align with the energy of your purpose.

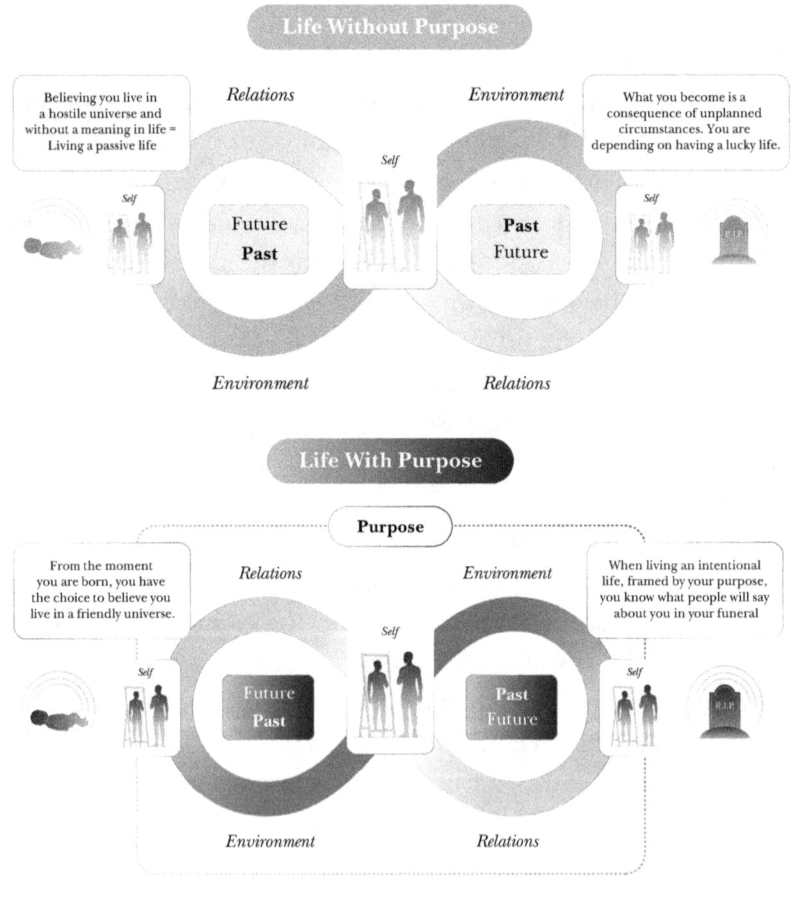

Figure 8

Align Your Communication with Your Intentions

In my assignment as president of Roche India, the new strategy's main objective was to empower the team to make more decisions, and with this added power came more responsibility. It also meant trusting each other, which is easier said than done. The team members with more authority had to trust the less experienced members to make mistakes and learn from them. The less experienced members had to trust that those with more authority had more authority because of their experience. The strategy also required excellent communication. We're used to hiding our mistakes so that others will have the "right impression" of us, and leaders are used to giving feedback only when things go wrong, but we needed a model of communication that would flow better, and that's what I implemented.

Meanwhile at home, a similar situation was playing out. By now our kids ranged in age from ten to fourteen, and we'd given them more responsibility to make their own decisions and we needed to start trusting them. But things didn't exactly get off to a smooth start. While attending a swimming competition in Jordan and staying with a host family, they broke every cellphone rule we had. Without us there to enforce the rules, they used their phones at the dinner table, didn't answer when we called, and stayed up late playing games on them. As a result, they weren't allowed to use their cells for a couple of weeks after they got home, and I let them know they wouldn't be allowed to take their cells on their next trip, to Nepal, scheduled for a month later.

"When I think of you three making wrong decisions when I am not around, I get very sad and worried," I said during a meeting I'd summoned them to in my home office. "Apparently, you didn't learn the importance of discernment and making the right decisions. I wonder what other wrong decisions you might be making. I'm trying to figure out how I can be a better mom. I love you, and I only want you to be happy, and you can only be happy when you learn to make the right decisions."

They nodded as if they understood, but they definitely *weren't* happy at that moment.

A few minutes later, fourteen-year-old Marco was back in my office with a request.

"Mom, can I *please* take my phone on the trip?"

It took me by surprise, but instead of shouting no, I decided to use generative listening— the technique of listening without debating, accepting what others are saying without judgment, with the goal of helping them build something greater than what I want or what they want.

"In principle you shouldn't. Every decision has its consequence, and as you decided to break the rules and had no discernment on the last trip, the consequence is clear. We need to avoid misbehavior with the next host family, and you have to experience the consequences of your bad decisions."

"Mom, I understand why you were disappointed, and I want to show you what I learned," he said. "But I'll only be able to show you if I take my phone with me. And if I don't answer your calls, don't tell you every place I am, and use the phone in the wrong way, you can take my phone and keep it for a month when I get back. But if I take it and prove that I learned, won't you feel very happy that you taught us right?"

I was very impressed by his thought process and the clarity with which he argued, but more than anything, I admired his proactiveness in suggesting an option that would prove he'd learned from the experience. If he didn't take his cell phone again, I wouldn't have the chance to find out that I could trust him. He gave me a chance to trust him instead of punishing him.

Long story short, he took his phone to Nepal and to this day he texts me wherever he is, and even if I don't answer, he tells me what he's doing and how he is. (His sisters didn't take their phones because they weren't sure they could honor the commitment—a display of responsibility and vulnerability that also impressed me.)

After this experience, I realized that Marco used Scharmer's *Theory U* model (see graphic below) to get what he wanted. He downloaded his past patterns, opened his mind and heart to what I felt, aligned what he wanted with what I wanted, and prototyped a solution. And then it occurred to me that this was exactly what my team needed to do at Roche. Both sides needed to be more vulnerable and compassionate like Marco was, opening their minds and hearts to each other.

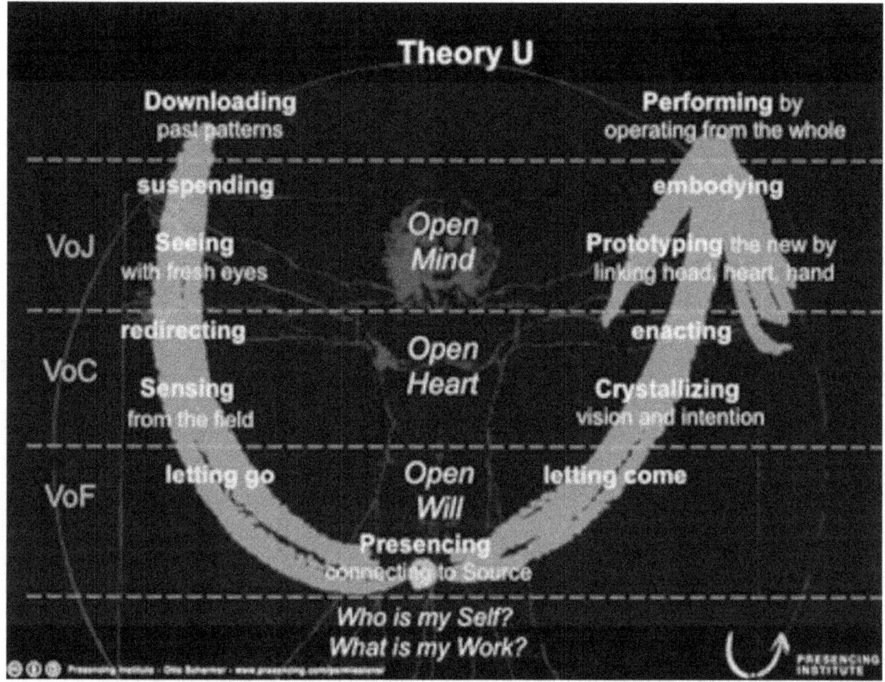

Figure 9

So I suggested that we start using a dialogue model by physicist David Bohm in which both parties would share their points of view and build something together, a simpler model with a similar outcome to Scharmer's *Theory U.* This model would help team members talk about their mistakes and their perceptions of them as well as their feelings and the stories behind them while also acting on them. It would also guide them to listen to each other receptively, knowing they all wanted the same general outcome.

The model, which follows, is based on the reframing model presented in the previous chapter, and it can help us create stories at work that will improve our focus on the collective purpose and leverage conflicts and difference in perspectives:

Each team member describes the event or situation from their perspective

Each one identifies the stories they created in the given situation

Each one identifies and describes their feelings about it

Each one shares what their intentions were

Together they agree on the actions that will bring them closer to the outcome they want to achieve (based on their collective purpose)

Then have the other party involved in the event or situation do the same so you can find a solution that satisfies what you both want.

Gaurav Patel, a brilliant professional who came to work with us, put the model into the simple graphic that follows (Thanks, Gaurav—you're amazing as both a professional and a human being!):

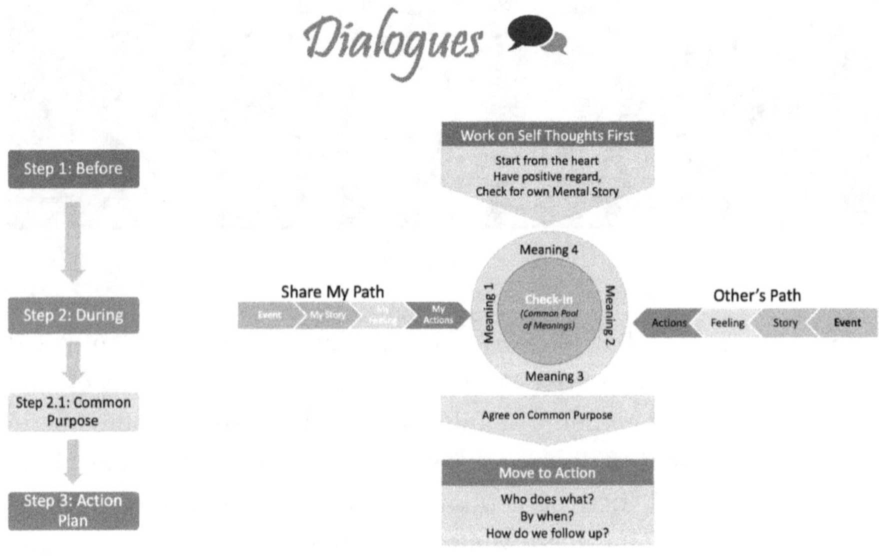

Figure 10

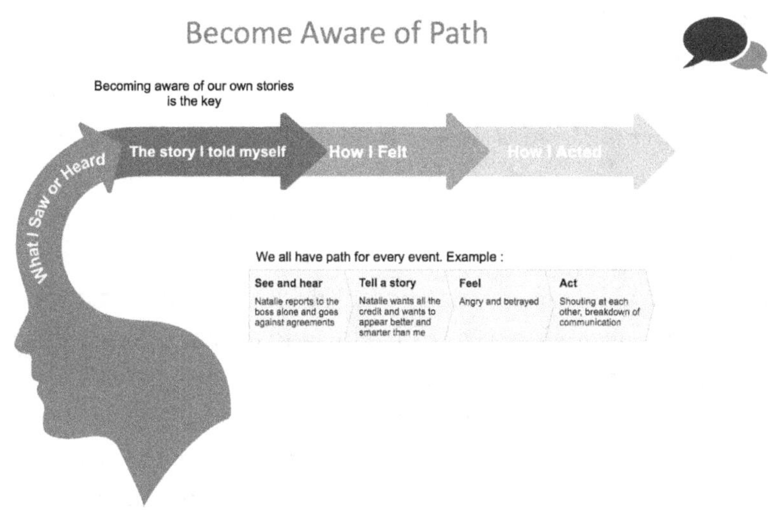

Figure 11

As the graphic shows, whenever we're doing or saying something, there's an underlying story, often one we haven't told others. We might not even *know* the story, which may become evident when we have to make a quick decision and consider only the words that others are using. We're likely to act based on our first reaction, probably an emotional one, and we may say or do something we wouldn't have consciously chosen to do. *Where did* that *come from?* we might wonder. But when we know the story behind the story and have told others about it, it's much easier to keep ourselves on track, and others can offer their help when we need it.

When our stories are clear to all, we can align our intentions with others' to achieve what we want. Most of the time, we're blinded by what we want to avoid. In my case, I could have been blinded by my desire to prevent my children from repeating the same mistakes they made with their phones, but my *ultimate* desire is to be a good mother and for them to have discernment and make the right decisions. I was able to step back, see the bigger picture, and tell them what I really wanted, and this allowed my son to help me achieve it. He developed his own version of dialoguing and determined the role he needed to play to make me a better mother while also making himself a better son and a better person in general.

Forming patterns based on experience is natural. These patterns help us come to conclusions we can base decisions on. These conclusions are the stories we're constantly building in our minds, and they're often the result of a mix of emotions and memories. In other words, they're not always based on reality, and when that's the case they can lead to biases and hinder our ability to make coherent decisions. (Remember how unconscious biases factor into our leadership and parenting styles, from Chapter 4?) But patterns are also related to survival. They can tell us whether we need to run or fight in a particular situation. And they make learning easier, serving as memory aids. Being conscious about the patterns we follow and being intentional about using the right ones in building stories clearly and communicating them will open important doors.

That's the first step in connecting our intentionality (right intentions + right motivations) with the integrality of our lives (our past, our future and the various systems in our lives), rewriting our storyline based on our intentions, our purpose. Knowing our purpose isn't enough. We need to be able to express it clearly and connect our intentionality and the integrality of our life. By rewriting our storyline, we'll create a new perspective on our past and our future that will help us achieve our purpose.

In the following exercise, we'll do just that.

Exercise 4 – Rewriting My Story Framed by the Life I Want to Live

---

Follow the instructions below for writing your story. And remember—it's based on how you want to live your life, not what you want to fight against.

Your Purpose

My purpose in life is:

____

Reframe past stories based on your purpose

Write the beliefs you've held about each part of your life (see example below), and then rewrite them so that they contribute to your purpose. Write about one lesson that each belief provided. You can expand your answers later.

Example:

Family

Old story: *I had a complicated family, with the divorce of my parents and a very purposeful but mostly absent father who had high expectations for my future. I thought he wanted me to follow into his profession.*

New story: *My complicated family and my parents' divorce taught me to deal with a diversity of thoughts and expectations. Not following my father's career path motivated me to find different ways to make him proud by being myself and standing up for what I liked and believed in. Seeing my father living his purpose showed me how I wanted to live my life.*

School

Old story: *I was different from other children and I was often alone. I didn't attend social gatherings often, as my mother was very strict and didn't allow us to go to sleepovers, parties, or concerts, and I had few friends. I fought against the status quo that said girls should like playing with dolls and not like reading or doing boys' activities. I was an unhappy child.*

New story: *Being different, I learned the importance of standing up for myself. Since my mother was very strict, I spent much more time with my family than with friends, which has helped me to be a good mother. My leadership skills surfaced early when I stood up for the things I believed in even if it might cost me friends or got me labeled as different. I was a child learning that happiness doesn't depend on your environment; it depends on you. Being conscious of who I was and living coherently according to who I am brought me happiness.*

Family

Old story: ____

____

____

New story with purpose: _________________________________

____

____

School

Old story: ____

____

____

New story with purpose: _________________________________

____

____

Love relationships

Old story: ____

____

____

New story with purpose: _________________________________

____

____

Myself/Who I am

Old story: ____

____

____

New story with purpose: ______________________________

____

____

Reframe Your Future with Your Purpose

Align your purpose with your role in each area of your life to determine your missions in those areas and list them below. The example that follows is for someone whose purpose is to bring new perspectives to others to identify unknown possibilities and prosper.

Family

My mission in my family is to share different ways of looking at events when talking with my husband or educating my kids and show them how this can help them succeed.

Work

My mission in my work is to always allow space for everyone's perspective to be shared openly, so others can see beyond their own beliefs.

Friends

My mission with my friends is to always find a way to share other perspectives when they're being negative or criticizing groups or ideas that aren't ours, showing them how this can broaden our possibilities.

Communities

My mission in my communities is to support voices that haven't been heard and ignite conversations incorporating their perspectives and providing a broader view of the situation.

World

My mission in the world is to always see different sides of a story and call them out in a way that celebrates diversity and the new possibilities that emerge from collective wisdom.

Family
My mission in my family is:

____

____

Work
My mission in my work is:

____

____

Friends
My mission with my friends is:

____

____

Communities
My mission in my communities is:

____

____

World
My mission in the world is:

____

____

Reframe your legacy with your purpose—create the ripple effect

Choose how you want to be remembered in each area of your life. What kind of impact did you have on your environment and relationships?

EXAMPLE:

Family

My family will remember me as a person who was intentional and lived coherently, guided by her purpose, and inspired others to do the same.

Work

My colleagues will remember me as a person who always spoke about her purpose and encouraged them to do the same, a person who was very coherent when making decisions and intentionally worked beyond her paycheck.

Family

My family will remember me as a person who:

____

____

Work

My colleagues will remember me as a person who:

____

____

Friends

My friends will remember me as a person who:

____

____

Communities

My communities will remember me as a person who:

____

____

World

The world will remember me as a person who:

____

____

Rewrite the Whole Story

Now bring it all together with your purpose story—the story that defines who you are and the impact you intend to make.

Example:

I am a person who believes in human beings and their infinite potential to connect and build a better world when their purpose drives them. I'm at my best when I can help others to see their purpose and unleash their potential. My purpose is to elevate humanity's consciousness by inspiring leaders to live a coherent life guided by their purpose so the world can be a better place.

I am a person who believes ____________________________

____.

I am at my best when______________________________
____.

The most important step to living in coherence is to be conscious of every situation and learn from it, being able to reframe any circumstance and get back on track toward living your purpose. For this you need to be aware and intentional about the stories you're constantly creating and telling yourself and others. Your plans might work differently from what you'd envisioned, but the important thing is to come back to your purpose and change direction. When you have a clear purpose and your emotions don't cloud your vision, you can change plans as many times as it takes to get back on track. No matter where life takes us, there are always opportunities within view to live your purpose, whether they're the ones we expected or surprises. Having this knowledge and experiencing it over time will give you confidence.

The transformation of knowledge and experience into wisdom is a skill you'll build by turning the theories behind integrality, intentionality, and coherence into practice. And when you share your wisdom with others, it will grow. Sharing what you learn with others leads to more learning. (We'll discuss this in more detail in Chapter 10.)

As for turning theory into practice, it's a very logical progression. As you'll see in the next chapter, it's really just a matter of habit, and once you see the benefits, it will happen naturally.

PILLAR THREE

COHERENCE

CHAPTER 8

WE CAN LEAD WITH LOVE BY BEING COHERENT

One of my directors used to be very hard on both himself and his team, and I heard he was hard on his family too. He told me he wanted to keep a certain distance from his people so that he'd be clearheaded enough to handle any situation, although I knew how much he cared about them. Over time he worked on his purpose and started to draw on his care and concern for others as a strength rather than hiding it like a weakness or fragility. He started to talk about his purpose and align his actions with his beliefs and his words, and his team eventually became one of the most engaged in the entire company and his results improved significantly.

The benefits extended to his family life too. In one of our routine morning coffees together at the office before the others arrived, he told me he'd hugged his twelve-year-old son the other day because he was proud of him for doing well on a test. He said he'd always been proud of him and told him so but used to keep a distance because he thought that if he expressed his positive emotions, he wouldn't be taken seriously when he needed to be strict. Like many people, he believed that to be respected in his position as educator and leader of the family, he had to avoid becoming too close. Recently, though, he'd started hugging his son and complimenting him more often. He started *showing* his pride in him, and his actions started to confirm his stories.

"I was surprised by his reaction and his drive to study more," he said, looking like he'd discovered a hidden treasure. "All just to get more hugs."

I had to laugh. "It *is* amazing, isn't it?"

"It really is. And even more amazing, since I'm living what I really am, it seems that life is flowing easily now. I feel lighter, and the care and love I express is coming back to me in a pretty nice way."

His happiness was obvious, and it warmed my heart to see it. His actions were becoming coherent with his beliefs, his values, and his thoughts.

Your actions have to confirm your stories. Knowing the difference between living what you want and living what you want to avoid is what makes living in coherence possible. When you tell strong, clear stories but keep avoiding things the way my director avoided closeness with others, this will create distrust and disbelief and you'll lose credibility. But when you know how to express your emotions—living what you believe during both the good moments and the bad, staying focused on your mission and purpose—you'll be modeling behavior that makes it easier for everyone to create deeper connections and understand each other.

Your stories should be a guide as you explore what life can bring you. They can be a foundation for intentionally unleashing what quantum physics calls "participatory universe" potential. Developed by Nobel Prize winner John Wheeler, the theory is that how we observe the world affects what it will become. It's known as the *observer effect*: the act of observing changes the phenomenon being observed.

Consider that in the context of what Einstein said: "The most important decision we make is whether we believe we live in a friendly or hostile universe." Knowing we aren't just observers of life but creators of the universe, we can understand that absolutely everything we do will have either a positive or a negative impact on the world. If we believe we live in a hostile universe, we'll keep fighting against something. We'll be in survival mode, defending ourselves from threats and bad outcomes. Limited by our fears, we'll create a limit to our lives and the possibilities that come our way. But if we believe we live in a friendly universe, we'll be motivated to create, to build, and to expand. There will be no limits to our capacity and creativity, and we'll reach our exponential potential.

If fear is the story behind our story, it will filter how we see reality, making threats more visible, causing more fear, and creating limiting beliefs—beliefs that impose limits on our lives. If love, care, and dreams are the story behind our story, it will filter the world differently, allowing us to see more opportunities and possibilities, live an abundant life, and inspire others to live the story with us. It's critical to learn how to live the right emotions. Constantly checking what's influencing you and how this in turn influences those around you will help you to live more consciously and reframe situations positively.

We can fulfill our missions in life by living the right emotions, the emotions that drive the kinds of happy endings we're seeking for our stories. But what *are* the right emotions? It's time to figure that out.

We Can Always Choose Constructive Emotions

A participant in a seminar asked me an interesting question: if one of my family members were murdered and the killer was present when I arrived at the scene, would I kill him or her? I answered that I wouldn't. I'm not a murderer, and killing another person would only add another layer of suffering to the situation. I want to live in a world of love and compassion, and I wouldn't want my children to see their mother as a murderer. I wouldn't want my husband to see me as capable of taking another human being's life. In this case, my rage, anger, and sadness wouldn't become destructive because they wouldn't drive my actions. Instead, by living my love for life and human beings, I would transform my negative emotions into constructive ones.

Express yourself completely,
then keep quiet.
Be like the forces of nature:
when it blows, there is only wind;
when it rains, there is only rain;
when the clouds pass, the sun shines through.
If you open yourself to the Tao,
you are at one with the Tao
and you can embody it completely.

If you open yourself to insight,
you are at one with insight
and you can use it completely.
If you open yourself to loss,
you are at one with loss
and you can accept it completely.
Open yourself to the Tao,
then trust your natural responses;
and everything will fall into place.
—Tao Te Ching, verse 23, by Lao Tzu, translated by Stephen Mitchell

Eastern philosophy and psychology don't see emotions as simply negative or positive—their significance is related to the choices we make and the actions we take when we experience them. An emotion can be destructive or constructive depending on the decision or action that accompanies it. We can make a negative feeling constructive if we're motivated to take compassionate, kind actions. Meanwhile, as psychologist Daniel Goleman explains in *Destructive Emotions: How Can We Overcome Them?,* Western psychology and philosophy *do* categorize emotions as positive or negative. Love, affection, and happiness are purely positive, and hate, anger, and sadness are purely negative. So Westerners are taught that it's good to feel love, affection, and happiness and that it's bad to feel sadness, anger, and hate. As a result, we feel guilty when we experience negative emotions, and we constantly strive to live a happy life filled with love.

In the East, it's okay to be sad or angry, but clinging to those emotions will create suffering and start to drive your decisions, which will become destructive. If you feel sadness and anger, ask: *What do I really want? How do I want this to affect me and influence others?* Then you can act with compassion and love, transforming the initial emotion into something constructive. At the same time, positive emotions can be destructive if you become attached to them and want to avoid losing them as opposed to simply living them. We suffer or feel pain whenever we make decisions based on fear of losing love, and those emotions inevitably turn destructive.

The behaviors resulting from constructive emotions are a strong basis for building resilience that allows us to live comfortably with vulnerability. And deciding to live with constructive emotions is a choice we can all make and a skill we can all develop.

Leaders Who Engineer Positive Epigenetics Build Healthier Environments, Systems, and Communities

Conversely, a leader who processes emotions constructively—transforming fear into learning, or anger into clarity—becomes an **engineer of positive epigenetics**, building healthier, more resilient, and more creative teams.

Knowing others is intelligence;
knowing yourself is true wisdom.
Mastering others is strength;
mastering yourself is true power.
If you realize that you have enough,
you are truly rich.
If you stay in the center
and embrace death with your whole heart,
you will endure forever.
—Tao Te Ching, verse 33, by Lao Tzu, translated by Stephen Mitchell
"We are what we think. All that we are arises with our
thoughts. With our thoughts, we make the world."
— The Dhammapada (verse 1)

In the late 1980s, an extraordinary dialogue began in Dharamsala, India, between the Dalai Lama and leading scientists, a collaboration that came to be known as the **Mind & Life Dialogues.** Visionaries such as Goleman, neuroscientists **Francisco Varela** and **Richard Davidson**, emotion researcher **Paul Ekman**, and Buddhist monk **Matthieu Ricard** came together to explore a profound question: "*How do emotions shape* *the mind, and can they be trained to cultivate resilience and well-being rather than suffering?"* These encounters challenged the Western view that emotions are simply "positive" or "negative" and raised the possibility that even fear, sadness, or anger can be transformed into **constructive forces** when met with awareness and compassion.

One of the most striking outcomes of these dialogues came from **Davidson's neuroscience research.** By studying the brains of experienced meditators, Davidson found that the cultivation of compassion and constructive emotions led to **measurable changes in brain activity,** especially in areas related to resilience and well-being. This was one of the first demonstrations of **neuroplasticity**—the brain's capacity to be reshaped by how we train our mind and process our emotions. As Davidson put it, *"Well-being is a skill."* And as Ricard reminded the scientific community, *"Happiness is a skill."* Both point to the same truth: the way we process our emotions isn't fixed—it can be learned, practiced, and shared.

This insight is profoundly relevant for leaders today. Our **language and behavior** aren't neutral; they're signals that influence the neuroplasticity of those around us. Over time, these signals become embodied in the people we lead, eventually even shaping their **epigenetic expression**—how their genes are turned "on" or "off" depending on the emotional climate they live in. A leader who operates out of fear and destructive emotions creates stress that can manifest in their teams as anxiety, burnout, and even physical illness. Conversely, a leader who processes emotions constructively—transforming fear into learning, or anger into clarity—becomes an **engineer of positive epigenetics**, building healthier, more resilient, and more creative teams.

The graph on **coherence** on page 158 shows this process as a journey over time. Experiences trigger reactions and actions, which then cascade into consequences. When leaders reframe, present themselves with vulnerability, and act with purpose, they open the door to resilience and meaning for both themselves and their teams. But when leaders remain stuck in fear of the future or attachment to the past, they touch off destructive cycles that could result in PTSD, depression, or chronic disengagement. It's like the old saying:

"Watch your thoughts, they become your words.
Watch your words, they become your actions.
Watch your actions, they become your habits.
Watch your habits, they become your character.
Watch your character, it becomes your destiny."

Figure 13 on the reframing of **constructive and destructive emotions** shows how the same experience can take two opposite paths depending on how it's processed. When leaders are too attached to the desire to cling to pleasure or reject pain, the result is suffering and heavy feelings. If leaders live months or years attached to destructive emotions such as fear, anger, or resentment, this becomes the emotional environment in which their people operate. With time, it transforms into an **epigenetic phenomenon**, influencing the health, creativity, and even the families of their employees. But when leaders reframe experiences as temporary and ask, *How will this help me when tough times come and how will it build my learning story?* they transform emotions into constructive energy. This reframing lightens the load for both the leader and their teams, creating space for peace, creativity, and growth. The science and wisdom now agree: Leaders literally shape the future biology and psychology of those they serve. See Figure 12.

As a leader, if you knew that the health of your team and their families was largely up to you, what would you choose? How would you be more intentional about the language you use and the behavior you model?

COHERENCE: BEHAVIOR + COMMUNICATION ALIGNMENT AND CONSISTENCY (ACTIONS + LANGUAGE)

Resonating to impact further

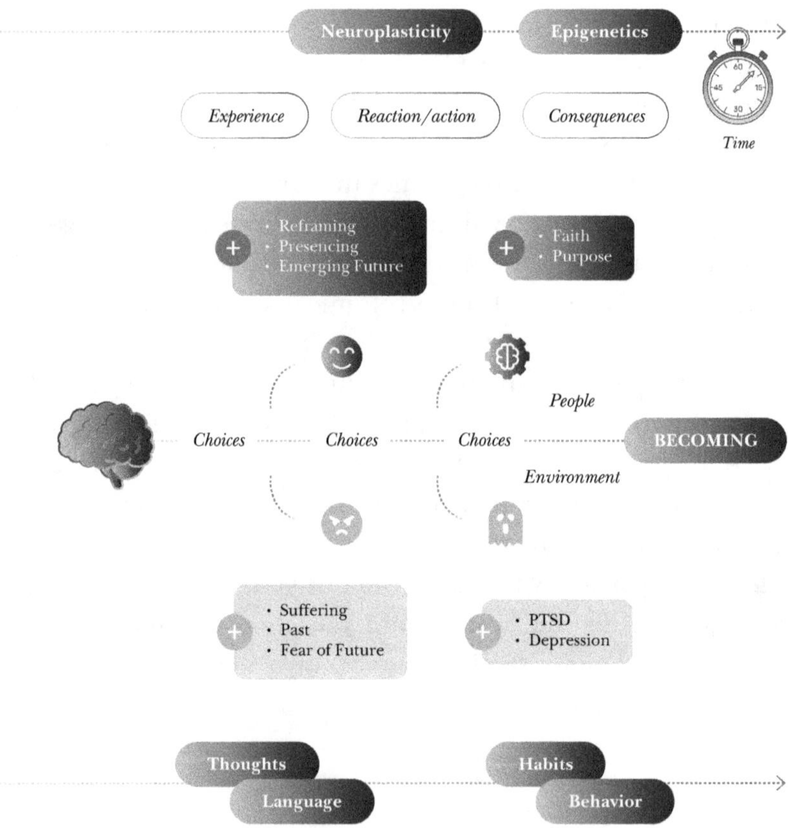

Figure 12

REFRAMING
DESTRUCTIVE EMOTIONS
INTO CONSTRUCTIVE EMOTIONS

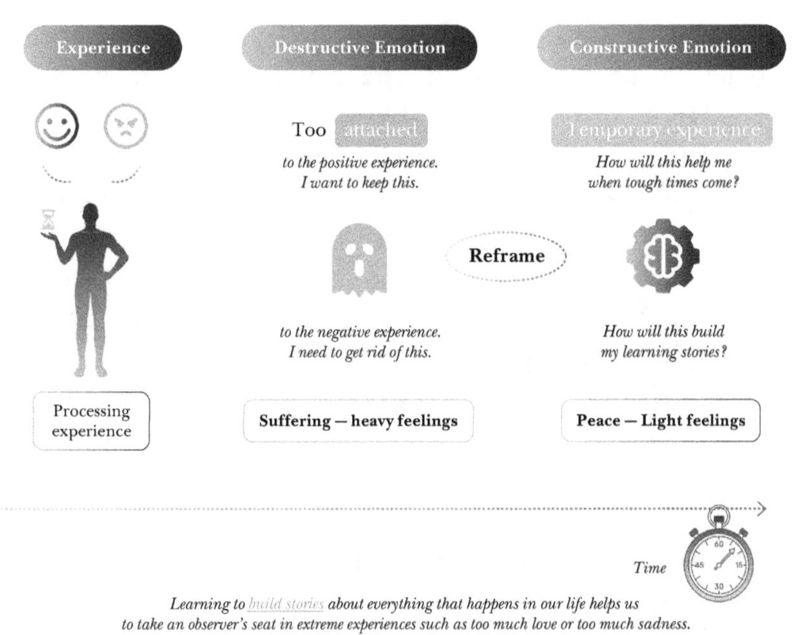

Figure 13

We Can Learn to Live Constructive Emotions

In Buddhist philosophy, the four noble truths are:

- the truth of suffering
- the truth of the cause of suffering
- the truth of the end of suffering
- the truth of the path that leads to the end of suffering

One of the people I coached sent me a text message between sessions saying he wanted to discuss a situation involving one of his directors. He's a company CEO, and he'd been struggling to become more accessible to his teams, mainly his leadership team. He wanted to bring the organization to another level where people could manage themselves and make decisions, but he feared giving up control, as he believed his people needed his orientation to make difficult decisions. He used to say his profile was that of an achiever and a pusher and that's what people were used to. On the other hand, I heard from his team members that if he used more compassionate language and trusted them more, it would make life much more comfortable for them. They believed that with the freedom to take more risks, creativity would bloom and results would improve, given that this was a highly skilled, purposeful team.

When we talked between sessions, my client (who I'll call Mario) told me he'd had a conversation with one of his directors (who I'll call Rogerio) and needed to follow up. He said Rogerio was never clear with him, and after expressing his concerns, he'd leave the conversation without further discussion. He said Rogerio was always making excuses to meet with important stakeholders alone and excluding him.

Mario and I had been working for a while on changing the emotions behind the assumptions on which he was basing decisions. He often visualized worst-case scenarios, and his decisions were all about avoiding them. He always expected the worst of people and was always prepared to fix their mistakes. To try to motivate them to perform better, he'd accuse them of always doing less than they could and use fear of losing their bonus or a promotion as a tool. The outcome was predictable. Despite good financial results, the team was constantly afraid of falling short of the "extra mile" he always asked them to go. Now, based on our discussions about the recent situation with Rogerio, he said he wanted to empower his people to become more autonomous. He acknowledged that he'd been making his team suffer for some time and wanted to demonstrate more trust and belief in his directors and devote more focus to their purpose. But he wasn't totally convinced he'd be able to make this shift in his behavior with the team, although he knew it would lead to better results than he'd been getting.

Meanwhile, I'd recently attended a Young Presidents Organization meeting where Peter Sorckoff, a brilliant expert in behavioral science, made a presentation about the Fogg Change Model, which is the basis of modern behavioral-change science. It maintains that to change any behavior, we have to have the right motivation, the ability to do it, and the right trigger to drive it (B=M+A+T; behavior change = motivation + ability + trigger). It turned out that in Mario's case, I'd been following the Fogg model without realizing it. He had the motivation to help his team implement the transformation he wanted in the company, and to develop the right abilities I worked with him to bring compassion to his decision-making process, mainly in managing people and complex situations. Having more compassion would help him see that using commitment and purpose was likely to be much more effective in motivating his team to go the extra mile than using fear. But that still left the trigger.

When I started working in India, the leadership—under the guidance of Maturin Tchoumi, a brilliant executive—were already working on improving their relationships with each other, and they introduced me to a concept that would change the way I led: unconditional positive regard (UPR). Introduced by Stanley Standal in 1954 and later popularized by Carl Rogers, it's the essence of a psychologist's acceptance and support of patients regardless of what they say or do, which is essential to empowering them to change themselves. In Mario's case, he needed to believe that his directors always had good intentions, that they wanted to add value and feel valued. And knowing how to behave with compassion and feeling unconditional positive regard toward the organization, he needed to make the right word choices in order for his intention to have the expected outcome. It was the perfect way for him to develop the ability to change his behavior.

To achieve this, we worked on a simple generative-question exercise.

"Mario, do you see the opportunity you have here?" I said during a Zoom session. "Tell me all your thoughts about this situation. Facts, feelings, everything."

He poured out all his frustrations with Rogerio.

When he finally stopped talking, I said, "What is it that you really want?"

He shrugged. "I want Rogerio to talk to me, and I want to understand the motivation behind his behavior."

"Why do you want this?"

"Because I don't know what he's thinking. When he leaves me in the dark, which is almost always, I have no idea how to help."

I nodded and asked him to tell me what the ideal outcome would be. Mario explained that he wanted Rogerio to talk to him and tell him what he was planning. If he knew what Rogerio was doing, Mario could focus on other things.

I said that if this was what he really wanted, he could start a conversation in a way that would allow Rogerio to tell him what he's thinking without suffering. "Try following our model: compassion, unconditional positive regard, seeing the friendly universe, and creating a generative dialogue, always focusing on the purpose."

> Compassion – unconditional positive regard - framing friendly universe – generative dialogue – focus on purpose

He thought about it for a while.

"Okay, how about this?" he finally said, looking uncertain. "'Rogerio, I know you have the best intentions and you want your team to strive together with the company. I have it in my head that you might be excluding me from meeting with the stakeholders and not knowing what you're thinking makes me anxious. I'd appreciate it if you'd share your thoughts with me, because I could just change my focus to another task instead of guessing what you're planning to do. In the end, we just want our product launch to succeed so our clients can benefit from them as soon as possible.'"

I wanted to hug him, but I had to settle for a huge smile. "Mario, you were compassionate but firm. You shared the story behind your actions. You expressed your feelings in a very compassionate way. You made the problem about you, not him. You're nurturing a generative dialogue, and you'll probably bring trust to your relationship with Rogerio. You see? By expressing your thoughts, you're modeling what you want Rogerio to do."

I could tell from his smile that he got it. "It feels good to trust my director," he said. "It feels right to show my own doubts and fears so that he feels comfortable expressing *his*. Do you think it will work?"

"There's only one way to find out."

A few days later, Mario talked with Rogerio for more than an hour about more topics than Mario had on his agenda. As a result, he decided to implement UPR and the process of generative-questions dialogue during all conversations with his team. As for Rogerio, he felt much more empowered and trusted. No longer feeling judged or afraid of being corrected by Mario, he started sharing the outcomes of all his stakeholder meetings with him.

Mario told me he started generative-question dialogues at home too, which led to a whole new kind of family dynamic. He'd come to understand that the reason any conversation reaches an emotional level and turns hurtful is that someone is suffering. Making compassion and unconditional positive regard the source of all thoughts and intentions makes it easier to create a generative dialogue because trust is built. Living constructive emotions builds a better life. It means harmonizing the mind and heart, balancing what you're thinking with what you're feeling, making it easier to live coherently. When you can do this, you've become a master!

Mario had started processing his experiences intentionally, choosing not to become attached to his feelings about experiences and to instead focus on the outcomes he wanted, the leader he wanted to be, and where he wanted to lead his organization. He learned to live more constructive emotions, inspiring others in his organization to live them too. Facing any moment of emotional decision-making with constructive emotions requires us to do each of the following:

- Bring compassion to the conversation
- Have unconditional positive regard
- Choose to live in a friendly universe

- Use generative dialogue—generative questions and generative listening
- Focus on the purposes of the individual and the organization (or family)

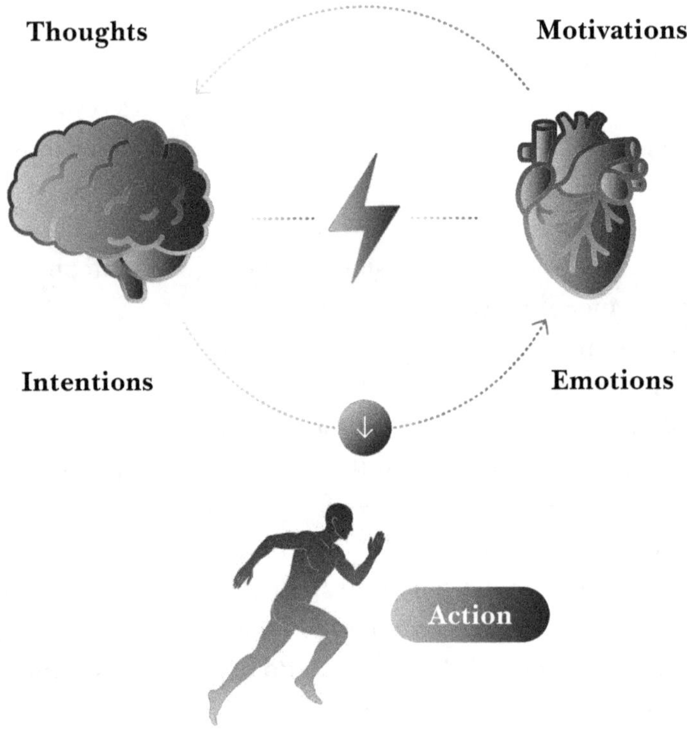

Figure 14

Of course, there will still be challenging times and situations, but you can express unconditional positive regard by differentiating the person from their decisions and actions. It's not the person you disagree with but the decision-making criteria that resulted in an objectionable action, and you can express what you don't like about their decision-making but still feel love for the person. Which brings us to the concept of loving vs. liking, as addressed by James C. Hunt in *The Servant.*

Love Improves Our Decision-making and Our Actions

Pro football coach Vince Lombardi once said: "I don't necessarily have to like my players and associates, but as their leader, I must love them. Love is loyalty, love is teamwork, and love respects the individual's dignity. This is the strength of any organization." In *The Servant*, Hunt takes the idea a step further. He says loving the team and each individual makes difficult moments easier to deal with and helps us make the right choices.

For leaders and parents, understanding that loving is an act of compassion can help *us* to be understood when we make decisions. When we use love in our language, we're using a nonviolent communication style that will make a huge difference in the outcome of everything we do. When we express love for children or coworkers in a conversation where we're calling out a decision or action we didn't appreciate, the listener will be more inclined to take corrective measures than to defend themselves. In other words, we make it easier for others to take steps toward a better outcome for both us and them.

At work, having the tough conversations is easier when we love our team, when leading people is a passion because we believe in human beings. We can communicate more compassionately, based on constructive assumptions, and help others think of solutions rather than feeling like they need to defend themselves.

We once had a manager who couldn't work with his team. The director had tried every way he knew to build a bridge, and the head of HR had tried coaching the manager to be a better leader, but they concluded that the team would never respect him. They also told me he had low self-awareness and difficulty receiving feedback. The company decided to let him go, as this would be best for everyone, including him. His image was deteriorating, and his poor people-management skills were overshadowing his technical expertise, the reason he had been promoted to manager. But during the separation meeting, he refused to go, and after a while I was asked to talk to him. When I arrived at his office, he was pale and stammered as he told me all the reasons he didn't believe he should have to go. In short, he didn't believe he was a bad professional.

"What would be the best way for you to succeed in your current position?" I asked.

"To give me a new team," he said without hesitation. "This one is already biased, so they'll never respect me."

I asked him how the new team would feel about him when they learned that the previous team was fired because they didn't get along with him. "How will your peers and the rest of the organization look at you then? Do you think they'll respect you for firing colleagues who were with the company more than fifteen years?"

"The employees might have a bad impression at first, and the new people might be scared when they start, but with time I can manage it."

"What other solutions might there be that will allow you to show your best side and be successful? Do you have the right environment to do that after so much history? If you were given a chance, how would you start over?"

"I'm *sure* I could show my best if the environment were different. I'd be much closer to my team. I'd listen more. I wouldn't control them so much." With excitement in his eyes, he went on with a list of things he'd do better if circumstances were different. But then a look of despair took over. Although he knew what he should do, he also knew it wouldn't be possible in the situation he was in, lacking the support of his team and peers.

But he was missing the fact that if he wanted different circumstances, he couldn't do better than to get a fresh start somewhere new. "Don't you want to give it another try at another company?" I said. "If you start from zero, you can be a great professional. Here you've become your past choices and attitude. If you start with a blank slate at a new company, you'll have the chance to show everybody you can lead a team. *I* respect you as a professional and a human being, though I'm not fond of some of the decisions you've made, and I can refer colleagues to you and help you with some leadership decisions for the next few months. I'll be there for you, I promise."

His eyes brightened and his shoulders relaxed. "Would you really recommend me? You have contacts at the pharmaceutical association—do you think I have a chance?"

"Yes, of course. I know what you're capable of, and I know the circumstances that brought you to this point. I would recommend you and also add coaching points any leader could help you with. I can call HR right now, and while you sign the papers I'll ask them to help me write a recommendation letter for you to leave with. And then we can keep in contact and I'll support you. How does that sound?"

I could see in his eyes what *he* was seeing: a new horizon. He was already envisioning himself starting over at a new company.

He picked up a pen and signed the papers.

In the weeks to come, I did recommend him to some colleagues, and he did land a management position at a new company where he went on to thrive. So the story had a happy ending even though his boss and the head of HR had become angry with him and regarded him as unprofessional. I believed in him and wanted him to be successful, and feeling that, he trusted me. And because he trusted me, he started making decisions based on his dreams instead of remaining stuck with the constant fear of losing his job. He reframed his fear into a desire to succeed again and was able to get through a difficult situation. And so was I. Instead of focusing on the fear that he might continue to create difficulty for the people answering to him, I believed he could do well elsewhere.

Love works the same way at home. In a family setting, it's crucial for parents to differentiate our love for our children from our dislike of their decisions. Teens often take parents' lack of patience and angry words as an excuse to say, "They don't like me, so whatever."

I've always told my kids how much I love them, and I also let them know when I'm not crazy about their decisions or choices. For example: "Son, I love you so much, but I get very angry when you decide not to be dedicated to your schoolwork and let your grades go down. You're always good at it when you *are* dedicated. What are you focusing on instead?" That way I guided him toward finding a solution and correcting himself without leaving room to think he was a bad student. And the belief that he was a good student helped him come up with good study patterns that brought him great grades in his last years of high school.

Meanwhile, although my daughter was always impeccable with her school notes, all neatly written with beautiful handwriting, her room was a different story. I wanted her to understand that this wasn't productive and that she had the neatness bug inside her, as her notes showed. "A messy room leads to a messy life," I told her, "and I wish your room was as neat as your school notes." I'd told her I loved her when I saw her notes, and I told her again in the same conversation as I told her I didn't like her messy room. After many attempts and repetition, it worked. She started making sure her room was neat before going to school in the morning. I'd tell her how much I liked her decision to organize it, and with time, she got used to keeping an impeccable room, even on days when she left for swimming practice at four thirty in the morning. She may not *always* keep her room impeccable, but the efforts she *is* making to live in an organized environment helped her in her Army basic training and will help her wherever she goes.

When we reinforce our love for our kids at the same time as we point out decisions we don't like, we speed up the learning process. I've heard parents say, "My kids are lazy. They aren't helping at home like they used to," "I hate teenagers. They're so moody and impolite," and "My son drives me crazy. He's addicted to video games." But "hating" your lazy child is a lot harder to deal with than loving them no matter what. Kids become what you say about them, so why not make your life easier by reminding them how amazing and loved they are?

The more constructive emotions we choose to live with, the better decisions we make and the better lives we build. When life challenges us with "teenage moments" or *any* moments that cause negative emotions, it's an opportunity to practice reframing them into constructive ones and to stay motivated to live our purpose with plenitude and peace. Every challenge we face, every difficulty we reframe, becomes the foundation of a deeper wisdom. With each experience, we grow stronger, more resilient, and more capable of building a happy and fulfilled life.

In the next chapter, we'll explore the **lifelong learning pillar**—the path that helps us *keep* transforming challenges into wisdom.

Introducing the Coherence Quotient®

As an invitation for deeper self-reflection, I've prepared the Coherence Quotient® assessment for you. This tool helps you look honestly and compassionately at your life through the lens of the four pillars of coherence: integrality, intentionality, coherence, and lifelong learning. By answering the questions, you'll gain clarity on where you are today in each pillar, where you may be aligned, and where dissonance might still be limiting your potential. Your personalized interpretation will offer practical suggestions for strengthening each pillar so you can live—and lead—with greater clarity, purpose, and coherence. I wish you a beautiful and transformative dive into your Coherence Quotient®. Just scan the QR code below.

PILLAR 4

LIFELONG LEARNING

CHAPTER 9

LEARNING AND CONTEMPLATING LIFE'S LESSONS ACCELERATES COHERENCE

"I asked for strength, and the Universe gave
me difficulties to make me strong.
I asked for wisdom, and the Universe gave me problems to solve.
I asked for prosperity, and the Universe gave
me a job and brains to work.
I asked for courage, and the Universe gave me dangers to overcome.
I asked for patience, and the Universe placed me
in situations where I was forced to wait.
I asked for love, and the Universe gave me troubled people to help.
I asked for favors, and the Universe gave me opportunities.
I asked for everything so I could enjoy life.
Instead, it gave me life so I could enjoy everything.
I received nothing I wanted,
I received everything I needed."
—Unknown author

Learning to live coherently is a marvelous thing. We feel a lovely sense of accomplishment as we look back at all the good decisions that have led us to this perfect moment. But that moment is no time to rest on our laurels. Everything is temporary, and our lives can change in an instant. When we think we've achieved stability because we've landed a great job or become engaged to the love of our life, that's just another beginning. We've just entered a new system that will add complexity to our lives. And down the road there may be promotions and children, which will mean more systems and more complexity. Becoming leaders, partners, and parents always takes the game to another level.

With each new system you become part of, you need to ask yourself these questions: *How has my integrality increased? How can I adapt my intentionality to continue living coherently, with my purpose and my actions aligned? How can I incorporate others' purposes into my own?* Constantly examining our lives and discovering how we achieved coherence in each part of our lives builds wisdom and is key to sustaining a coherent life. We need to be lifelong learners to maintain a life driven by purpose.

When my mother gave me a copy of *The Servant* when I landed my first general manager position, she told me the book would guide me to do well by doing good. She told me that as a leader, I'd be responsible for many lives and families and that my life wasn't about me anymore. She told me I should be able to recognize the outcomes that my choices and behavior have on the people and the environment around me and recognize the lessons to be found in it all. That's the key to being a good leader, she said. Inside the book she left a bookmark printed with the poem I shared in the beginning of this chapter.

At that moment, I understood that like being a parent, being a leader is about transforming ourselves into better human beings and being in constant learning mode. We should always be able to connect the dots and learn from the past. We should always create visions and missions to share with others and build a better, aligned vision that also incorporates *their* perspectives; the collective perspective is always strongest. And I also understood that I had to learn to connect the dots to the *future*, aligning my intentions with the integrality of my life.

After you've understood and are conscious about the integrality of your life, the systems of your life, and the stories you decide to tell, you need to identify the intention you're living. That's when you achieve coherence in all systems of your life and it seems that the universe is conspiring in your favor. That's also when you need to be ready for the universe to give you what you want, probably in disguised forms. You'll need to be ready to keep learning—specifically, learning how to handle all the blessings you've been given.

Looking back on my life, I can see that every challenge came as a disguised blessing. When I left my country and my mother, not knowing if I would see her again, it was one of the hardest decisions I ever made, but it opened the path for me to pursue my purpose and discover the strength that comes from living far from everything familiar. When I faced the failure of my first marriage, I thought I'd lost everything, but in truth it was the doorway to build the relationship I really wanted to have. When I had to surrender to infertility, it felt like defeat, but the greatest gift of all came from that surrender: the most beautiful family I could have ever wished for.

The same happened in my professional life. Leaving the job I loved at the height of my success was painful and confusing, but it was only by letting go that I could step into a new life, filled with more purpose, impact, and fulfillment than I'd ever dared to dream of. If I'd followed only the emotions of those moments—fear, pain, and attachment—I wouldn't be who I am today, nor would I have the prosperity, family, and coherence that bless my life now.

I've learned to tell my stories with **intention**, conscious of the person I want to become and the future I want to help build. Of course, life will never look exactly as I picture it, but I'm absolutely certain that it will be better than anything I could have planned. When we show the universe—or God or life itself or whatever you want to name it—through our behavior and language that we're willing to be good, to do good, and to serve, doors begin to open. The signs are placed before us, sometimes in ways we'd never expect.

When my boss offered me the job of heading Bayer Pharma in Hungary when I was only thirty-two, I never would have thought of myself for such a role, but my boss did, and that's how the universe works too. It sees our potential, our willingness, and our readiness. It shows us where we're needed and what we're capable of. Our task is to read the signs, to accept the disguised blessings, and to keep learning as we move forward. That's the essence of lifelong learning: transforming challenges into wisdom, living with integrality, practicing intentionality, and holding our purpose with coherence, trusting that every experience is shaping us into who we're meant to become.

Lifelong Learning Allows Coherence to Flow through Life

At a certain point in our lives, we might reach a level where we believe we're coherent and balanced. Naturally, when that's the case, we don't want anything to change. We just want to maintain the balance and harmony. But that's not how it works. We stay balanced and coherent by leading dynamic lives in which we grow through change and the learning curve that requires.

When I was in Hungary, I was practicing yoga daily and bringing an ethical transformation to my company while also working with CEOs of other pharma companies to raise ethical standards in the market. At the same time, thanks to a psychiatrist-trainer who introduced meditation and inner development to our team, I felt deeply balanced and fulfilled. But then life reminded me that coherence is never static. In the same year, my mother passed away, my marriage ended, and Bayer announced a merger that threatened my position. It was one of the toughest periods of my life. Immersing myself in yoga and the teachings of the Vedas, I slowly learned to embrace change with equanimity. To my surprise, instead of losing everything, I was appointed GM. What looked like a year of loss became one of the richest years of growth in my life.

Later, when I was reassigned to Mexico, I carried this new perspective with me. What began as a professional move soon brought an unexpected twist: I reconnected with a past love, we married, and after the pain of infertility, we built the family I'd always dreamed of through adoption. Looking back, I see that none of these blessings would have come without the challenges that preceded them.

Bad things don't happen in our lives. Certain *situations* happen, and the stories we create about them will build the foundation for our future. Moments are just moments. Even if they inflict pain, it's what has to happen for me to achieve my purpose. Anything that happens is exactly what I need. It might not be what I wanted, but it's what I asked for. Somewhere along the way of experiencing divorce, losing my mother, and generally coping with fear and loss over many years, a bridge was built to bring me where I needed to be.

Each change we face comes with doubts and uncertainty and the feeling that life was easier before. We miss the "old times." But a beautiful moment occurs when we understand that changes happen so we can leverage them for our spiritual growth. At that moment, we start to see the importance of each step we've taken in our lives and learning from challenges. When we recognize life as a never-ending cycle of change, learning, growth, and enjoyment, we appreciate the importance of being lifelong learners. When we can see how our integrality is expanding within this cycle and maintain our focus on the purpose in each part of our lives, we'll finally achieve the coherence we're striving for.

The Cycle of Spiritual Evolution Is Completed with Knowledge and Experience

During a Vipassana yoga retreat I once attended, one of the discourses we listened to in the evenings included this parable told by the late S.N. Goenka, the world's leading Vipassana teacher and founder of the Vipassana Research Institute:

Once a young professor was traveling on a ship. He was a highly educated person with

a long tail of letters after his name, including multiple PhDs. But he had little experience of life. On the same ship was traveling an illiterate old sailor. Every evening the sailor would come to the professor's cabin to listen to his lectures. One evening as the sailor was about to leave, the professor asked the sailor, "Old man, do you know geology?"

"What is that, sir?"

"It is the science of the Earth on which we are living."

"Sir, I have never been to school. I have never studied geology."

"You have wasted a quarter of your life," the teacher said.

The old man left with a long face. *If such a learned person says so, it must be true,* he thought. *I have wasted a quarter of my life.*

The next evening, the professor was delivering a lecture on oceanography. At the

end of the session, the professor and the old sailor had a conversation like on the previous day.

"Do you know oceanography?" the professor asked.

"What is that, sir?"

"It is the science of the ocean on which we are traveling."

"No, sir, I haven't studied oceanography."

"You have wasted two-quarters of your life," the teacher said.

This time the old man left with an even longer face. He thought, *If such a learned person says so, I have wasted two-quarters of my life.*

The next evening, the professor delivered a lecture on meteorology. At the end of the session, he asked the sailor, "Do you know meteorology?"

"What is that, sir?"

"It is the science of the weather, wind, and rain."

"No, sir. As I have told you earlier, I have never been to any school or college. I don't know meteorology."

"You are staying on this Earth but don't know geology," the teacher said. "You are earning your living from the ocean, but you don't know oceanography. You deal with the wind, rain, and weather every day, but you don't know meteorology. You have wasted three-quarters of your life."

The old sailor was very unhappy this time. *When such a learned person says that I have wasted three-quarters of my life, I must have wasted three-quarters of my life.*

The next day the ship hit a rock, and the old sailor ran to the professor's cabin. Then he thought about the conversations he and the teacher had been having, and he came up with a question of his own.

"Professor, do you know swimology?"

"What is that, old man?"

"Do you know how to swim?"

"No, I don't know how to swim."

"Professor, you certainly have wasted *all* your life. The ship has hit a rock and is sinking. Those who can swim can go to the nearby shore. Those who can't swim will drown."

The teacher at the Vipassana retreat said that for us to get the full benefit of meditating, we had to understand the science behind it, but we also had to actually meditate. Intellectual knowledge isn't the same as really knowing something. To acquire true knowledge, you need to experience it.

When we're on the path of growth and learning, we often look for books or courses to support our development. Sometimes we underestimate the importance of our experiences and observations in different areas of our lives. Yoga teaches that the path to true growth should come from the balance between knowledge and experience. Without experience, knowledge is only words and skills—"knowledge obesity," as one of my mentees put it. On the other hand, experience without the proper knowledge doesn't support the growth we need. A conscious experience is key.

And the greater the *diversity* of experiences we seek out, the better. The effort to broaden our horizons can make a profound difference in our work outcome. For example, parents dedicated to raising their kids properly and educating themselves toward that end will become marvelous leaders. Being a parent involves helping children face challenges that appear every year in the new systems they become part of and the emotional changes that come with them. Parents who learn to support their children emotionally and help them make the right choices will be highly prepared to lead teams and help grow companies to achieve their purpose. At the same time, challenges involving their work teams can help them become better parents when the learnings are profound and reflective enough. Remember the story of one of my directors who learned to deal with his team with more compassion and then took the same approach with his son? The more systems you're part of, the more experiences you and those around you will benefit from. Becoming an expert in a certain area can have great value, but a diversity of conscious experience is critical to the lifelong learning that allows us to live coherently.

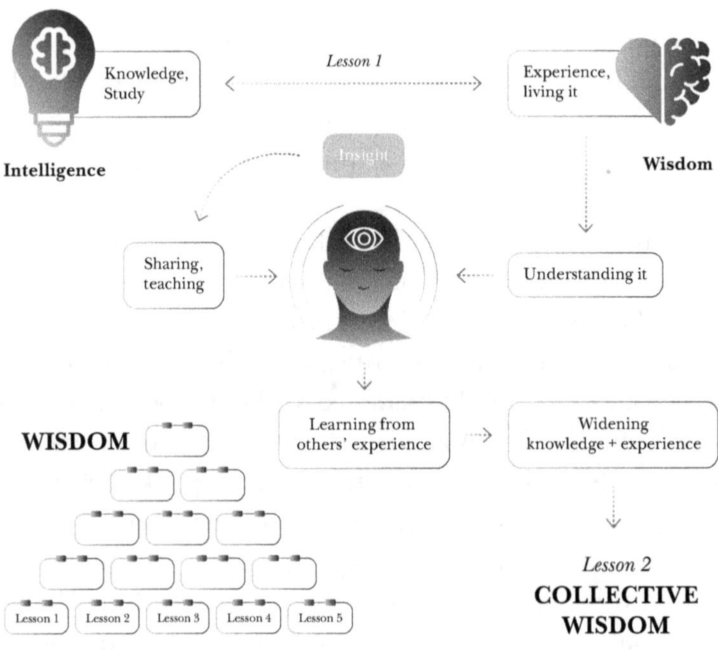

Figure 15

We Can Connect Dots Forward, Not Just Backward—Sorry, Steve Jobs!

In Steve Jobs' commencement address at Stanford University in 2005, he talked about his decisions to drop out of college but drop back *in* to take a calligraphy class, which factored into the quality of Apple's Macintosh computer ten years later. "It became the first computer with beautiful typography," he said. He hadn't known at the time how the class would help him, but he was able to connect the dots after the fact: "You can't connect the dots looking forward; you can only connect them looking backward. So you have to trust that the dots will somehow connect in your future. You have to trust in something—your gut, destiny, life, karma, whatever. This approach has never let me down, and it has made all the difference in my life."

For years, I believed we could only connect the dots by looking backward. But between reading Jobs's commencement speech and Otto Scharmer's *Leading from the Emerging Future,* I came to realize that we can also connect the dots *forward.* We can build on what we want to create.

Joseph Jaworski, in *Synchronicity: The Inner Path of Leadership,* explored this same mystery of how our lives unfold through unseen connections. He discovered that when we act from a deep sense of purpose and openness, circumstances and people begin to align in ways we could never have planned. His journey showed that leadership is less about controlling outcomes and more about surrendering to the unfolding potential of life itself. Jaworski called this "living in synchronicity," the state where inner intention meets the world's emerging possibilities—exactly what Scharmer would later describe as *presencing.*

Introduced in *Theory U,* presencing is being present in the moment while sensing what's emerging. This is especially important for people dealing with complex life and professional scenarios and constant change. When we connect the dots forward, we need to feel comfortable with uncertainty. We need to feel comfortable stepping onto a bridge under construction. We need to be comfortable breaking with the way we lived in the past.

In *Theory U,* Scharmer says we're presencing when we enter into communion with another person's intention, when we connect with someone by sharing observations about the past and focusing on what we've learned. When we both talk with an open heart and an open mind about a situation that brought us to a determined moment and align what we want by letting go of our individual thoughts and embracing a common dream, wish, or vision, a world of possibilities opens up. When we have a common vision and clarity on an outcome we can work toward, our minds and hearts see realities we wouldn't otherwise notice. Coincidences known as serendipities or synchronicities will start to happen, and your ability to see these opportunities while facing significant changes is a measure of your ability to connect dots forward and live a coherent life.

When we know system thinking, we know how systems are connected and the importance of seeing our lives as a network of systems. When we've created a vision for ourselves, our families, our communities, or our teams and we talk about it, hints about our vision and new perspectives will appear in places we didn't expect. Others will start to share their views, and their views might be the missing piece of our purpose. When we see our life as a whole and bring a systemic view to our lifelong learning process, the potential for learning growth is immense. And so is the potential for realizing our vision.

In India, we transformed Roche's operating model and business strategy, but we changed even more as human beings. I brought the essence of Danah Zohar's work from *Quantum Leader* to the table, along with Scharmer's *U Theory* and other teachings from various philosophies. With the help of our HR director, Swati Yadav (one of the most brilliant human beings I've met), we brought the training I designed for the Venezuelan team to the Indian team, and it eventually cascaded through the whole organization. Everyone participated in purpose and self-awareness exercises and learned how to change their methods of collaboration. As an organization, we translated the company's global purpose into a local vision.

To make it possible to see the emerging future, we put our vision and purpose into everything we did, and the serendipities rolled in. I can't recall how many times we were trying to work out the details of a particular strategy and we'd get a phone call, a visit, or a message that gave us exactly what we needed. One day we were sitting in my office, talking about new ideas, when I noticed that one of our directors was looking out the window, astonished. "Lara, look at the name they put on the new building." When I turned to look at the twenty-story building under construction a few blocks away, I saw that letters had been installed along a strip above the top floor, spelling out *SERENDIPITY*.

Figure 16

Many of us don't believe in serendipity unless it's right there in front of us, like that building. My husband used to say that every time he was worried about paying the bills at the end of the month, he'd end up being able to pay them but only just barely. But when he was pursuing knowledge and a better environment for his team and his clients, significant rewards would come his way, like a new client or a new employee with exactly the skills he was looking for. When what motivates us is greed or fear—fear of not making it to the end of the month, for example—we prevent ourselves from working from a place of love and higher service, which is where opportunities come from. When we have a clear vision for realizing our purpose, we live it in all systems of our life and we live with the right motivation—to serve a greater good—and when that's the case, we need to understand that absolutely everything that happens serves our purpose and accept the responsibility of learning from each experience. All it takes is to open our minds and perceive opportunities instead of problems. And when we inevitably see serendipities and synchronicities, it's a sign that we're on the right track.

No technology can compete with the power of a clear vision when it comes to uniting others toward a common goal and leveraging collective wisdom to see further and broader. Technology will never replace human consciousness and our power to connect systems through deeper relationships and purposes, but we can *harness* technology to benefit us as humans and the systems we're part of. It can help us optimize those systems to solve problems or fulfill needs that emerge with the dynamics of the fourth revolution, the technology revolution of the twenty-first century.

But what about the fifth revolution—the collaboration between human and machine intelligence, guided by humanity's values? We need to understand what's coming in order to make the future part of our purpose-realization journey. Living in coherence with the future is the only way to capitalize on the wonders it will bring.

Our Future Requires Lifelong Learning

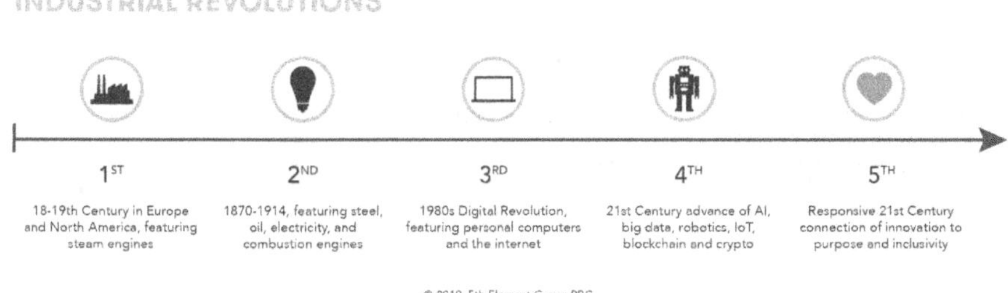

Figure 17

The changes we'll face in the next five to ten years will be scary or appealing, depending on how we act. To make the most of the opportunities headed our way, we'll need to live in a way that we can sense the emerging future and be the people shaping the future. Those who oppose the changes will resist them and won't be prepared, and they certainly won't prevent those changes from happening. But those who embrace the future can leverage the changes and create an environment where stress created by uncertainty is minimized and people can strive together to live their purposes.

Futurists like Ray Kurzweil—an American inventor and author known for his predictions on artificial intelligence, biotechnology, and the concept of "the **singularity**" (the point where AI surpasses human intelligence)—can see the future because they aren't afraid. They want to understand what's coming. And many want to help humanity see it faster and work toward it by using collective wisdom. When I was in Hungary, I started using a phrase in meetings and presentations that, by now, everyone who knows me has heard: "Cowards and heroes both have fears. The difference is that the heroes make decisions based on their dreams." In this new era that we face, the leaders will be those who can visualize a future where humanity can develop the consciousness to make the most of the immense changes that technology such as AI and quantum computing will bring. The leaders will be those who are adaptable, flexible, and have a clear purpose in life. They'll be able to evolve their purpose and their vision with each new challenge the new world dynamics present. They'll be able to develop products and services that offer solutions to the environmental destruction and lack of consciousness that we've lived with for centuries.

In the next chapter, we'll see how conscious human beings with clear purposes will *become* those inspiring leaders.

PART THREE

THE PROMISE OF LIVING AND LEADING WITH COHERENCE

CHAPTER 10

INSPIRING LEADERS ARE CONSCIOUS HUMAN BEINGS

The year was 2008. Paul Polman, incoming CEO of Unilever, was in Mumbai attending a celebratory dinner for his predecessor at the Taj Mahal Palace Hotel. Amid the clinking of glasses and warm introductions, a chilling sound shattered the night: gunfire. The hotel was under siege by terrorists.

Chaos erupted and guests scrambled for cover. But amid the panic, a different kind of story started to unfold—a story of courage and selfless service. Hotel staff from young banquet managers to veteran waiters transformed into protectors, ushering guests to hidden rooms and forming human shields, some of them sacrificing their lives to ensure the safety of others.

Witnessing these acts of bravery firsthand, Polman saw the profound impact businesses could have not just on profits but on society itself. The dedication of the Taj staff, their willingness to put themselves at risk for complete strangers, started a fire in him, and he emerged a changed leader. The Mumbai attacks became a turning point, forcing him to confront the limitations of a purely profit-driven business model. He began to see the need for a broader purpose and a commitment to social responsibility and sustainability.

This newfound purpose translated into action. Under Polman's leadership, Unilever embarked on an ambitious "sustainable living plan" aimed not just at financial growth but also at reducing the company's environmental footprint and making a positive social impact. The plan proved to be a success. Unilever's sales soared and the company became a beacon for businesses seeking to do good while doing well. Polman himself became a leading voice in the fight for a more sustainable future.

Today, Polman is known for being a CEO who's lived his purpose, brought it to the companies he's worked for, and, after stepping down as CEO, kept working toward his purpose. His social venture, called Imagine, trains executives in sustainable human-centric leadership. As co-author of the book *Net Positive: How Courageous Companies Thrive by Giving More Than They Take,* he says businesses have the power and the responsibility to move beyond profit and create significant positive value for the planet.

Polman's private and professional lives intertwined with the same objective: to do good for both society and the planet. Two missions, one objective. Besides inspiring the hundred thousand employees who worked for Unilever during his ten years as CEO, he was one of the drivers behind the UN's Sustainable Development Goals, which have been guiding governments and businesses to work together to address issues such as gender and income equality, clean water and energy, hunger, and climate change.

Polman lives his purpose beyond his selfish desires and in coherence. During his time at Unilever, many companies were talking about doing less harm and creating corporate social responsibility departments, but he dared to go beyond doing less harm and actually did *good* for society and our planet. He started a movement that changed the business world forever.

Polman became an icon among purposeful and impact-driven leaders because he knows who he is and what he wants and makes this clear in all areas of his life. His stories are reframed to serve his purpose—to serve the greater good. Seeing the integrality of his life, he considers the planet, society, communities, people, his team, and their families in his decisions instead of looking only for profit and short-term revenue increases or shareholder value. Because of this strategy, he brought coherence to Unilever and to many systems around it. And by the time he left the company, it was ready for whatever the future held because its purpose is future-focused. As a result, Unilever has become one of the most attractive multinational corporations in terms of both investment and employment.

During his decade of leadership, Unilever's market value more than doubled, its operating margins improved, and it became one of the most respected companies for sustainability and purpose-driven growth, and the seeds Polman planted are continuing to bear fruit. Today the company is recognized not only for its financial resilience—with sales growing 3.4 percent in the first half of 2025—but also for the coherence between its values and its strategy. Unilever is refining its portfolio, investing in high-impact segments, and maintaining the long-term vision Polman instilled. His legacy endures in every product, every initiative, and every decision that prioritizes people and the planet alongside profit, proving that when leaders live their purpose with coherence, their impact transcends their time.

But Polman's coherence did not end at Unilever. His systemic view of leadership has always extended beyond a single organization. While leading Unilever, he worked closely with Professor John Ruggie to advance and implement the United Nations Guiding Principles on Business and Human Rights, helping translate global frameworks into corporate responsibility and practice. For him, sustainability was never a marketing strategy—it was governance, accountability, and moral architecture embedded into the way business operates.

His commitment to systemic change also took form through impact investing and long-term capital allocation aligned with societal value creation. He has consistently advocated that financial markets reward companies that create net positive impact rather than pursue short-term gains.

Beyond corporate leadership, Polman co-founded initiatives such as The Valuable 500, mobilizing global businesses to place disability inclusion at the heart of their strategies. Through One Young World, he has supported and mentored a generation of emerging leaders committed to social and environmental transformation. His involvement in organizations such as the Saïd Business School at Oxford and other university boards reflects his belief that shaping future leaders is inseparable from shaping future systems.

Even in deeply personal initiatives, such as the founding of Kilimanjaro Blind Trust Africa, his coherence is evident: service is not a corporate posture but a life posture.

Seen through this wider lens, Polman's life illustrates a crucial truth: coherent leadership is not confined to a company's walls. It is expressed across institutions, capital markets, education, civil society, and personal action. It is systemic by nature.

Anyone who strives to be a conscious human being with a clear purpose will inspire others through his or her coherent way of living. They'll become great leaders even if that wasn't their goal. Whether we're parents, bosses, managers, supervisors, friends, or colleagues, we'll all be leaders at certain moments, and our most important task as leaders is to help our people become better human beings. In becoming leaders, we take on the responsibility of nurturing *others'* journeys to leadership—just like Polman did at Unilever and continues to do through Imagine. But instead of thinking about the weight of that responsibility, think of the happiness and fulfillment you can spread by sharing what you've learned. By modeling how to intentionally live your purpose, you'll inspire others to become conscious leaders and human beings, and they'll pass on what *they've* learned, elevating the cycle of consciousness.

Coherence Elevates Our Consciousness

For much of my life, I had to keep Lara the executive and the spiritual Lara separated. I was very fulfilled by my career and loved it, but I was also learning ancient philosophies and yoga and seeking a more meaningful life, and there were few people with whom I could talk about what I was learning. I was living alone in Hungary and my philosophy buddy, my mother, had passed by then. I was living a life of dissonance rather than resonance.

The solution I came up with was to bring spirituality to the corporations I worked with. During an annual conference, I led some optional yoga exercises in the morning and meditation sessions at the end of the day, and they turned out to be a hit. The morning sessions were well-attended, and *everybody* turned out for the meditation.

That conference brought my life into resonance. When I was able to talk about yoga and meditation and bring my whole self to the workplace, others appreciated it and we grew closer. But the most amazing thing I learned was the difference between experiencing moments of consciousness and changing your level of consciousness. When I started to live my spirituality at work and talked about it, my level of consciousness increased, and it transformed forever how I lived and worked. Finally, I fulfilled my promise to my mother: I'd brought spirituality to the workplace.

Real transformation will happen when we live more consciously every time a new challenge presents itself and live our purpose in all aspects of our lives. Every time we learn how to face a new challenge or a new system that's been added to our lives and can do it guided by our purpose, we step up our level of consciousness.

Our journey of becoming more conscious and living a coherent life consists of constant work on the four pillars of my WorkCoherence model: integrality, intentionality, coherence, and lifelong learning. As shown in the illustration below, the cycle of consciousness is a spiral because it keeps repeating itself and we keep growing our consciousness as we acquire more tools to deal with new systems and challenges entering our life. When we live the four pillars, we find ourselves developing greater self-awareness, living meaning-driven lives, having insights that guide our consciousness journey, resonating with all our systems, connecting the dots in our lives, and generally living harmonious lives.

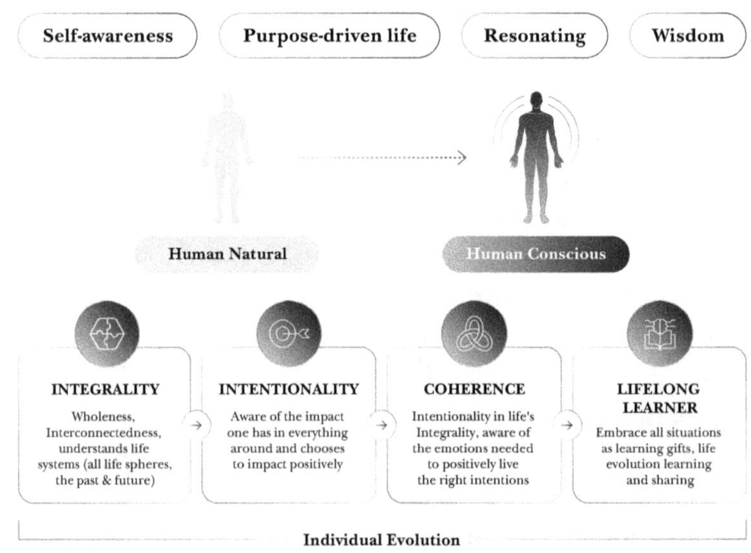

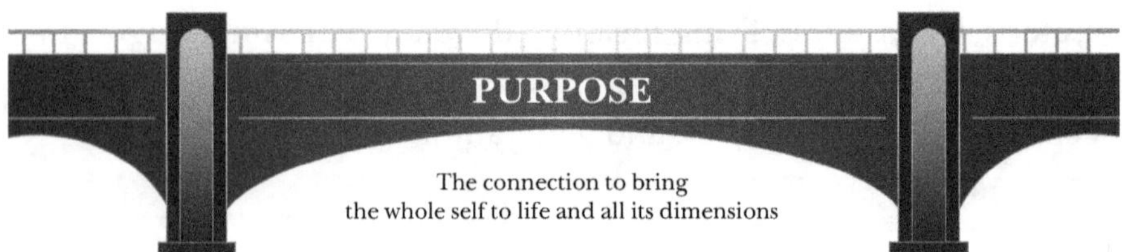

Figure 18

That said, there will always be things that disturb our harmony. We'll feel anger and frustration when our kids do wrong, when a boss behaves badly with us, or when our partner has a bad day and takes it out on us. Even a great promotion or news that you're expecting a baby will challenge the organization and routine of your life. But these are all opportunities to learn, grow, and step up to the next level of consciousness, provided you know how to use all the tools you acquired on the previous levels. And the higher our consciousness level, the more people we'll influence or have the chance to bring with us.

When our intentions are aligned in all systems in our life, a decision in one area of our life will influence other areas. The higher our consciousness, the broader the influence and impact we'll have. At this point, there are certain questions we'll ask ourselves:

- Why am I doing what I'm doing, and why am I not doing what I'm not?
- What do I want to leave to the world?
- What are people saying about me?
- When and why do people call me?
- In what circumstances do I lose track of time and things just flow?

In the search for these answers, we'll find our *ikigai*, our reason for living, and our purpose will start to unfold.

Coherent Leaders Share Their Story and Their Purpose

Indra Nooyi, the first woman of color to run a Fortune 50 company as CEO, led PepsiCo for twelve years, paving the way for it to become the world's second-largest food and beverage company. In the process, she inspired more than 260,000 employees. She was always very clear about her leadership style, and one of her trademarks was a process called PwP: performance with purpose. In an interview with NDTV in 2021, she explained it:

> *It was time to change hard cold-heartedness to performance with purpose. I wasn't trying to be soft or work on the hard numbers. I was trying to future-proof the company. I wanted our company to be successful into the future and not get into any trouble in societies or countries because of the business model we had. So my articulation of performance and purpose was not about giving money. We made a way for certain causes. It*

was "What if we changed the way we made money? What if we created a company where we cut costs by doing the right things for society? And we did the right things for society so that society would give us a license to operate?" We would be successful well into the future.

When her methods were criticized for being different and disruptive, she stood her ground, confident in her purpose. She never wavered in her commitment to "do the right things for society." And the results she got speak for themselves. Before she took over, the company's return was minus 1.25 percent, and in her first six years it grew to 28 percent. She also significantly changed PepsiCo's business model. The company had Pepsi and Frito-Lay plants around the world, some of them in water-distressed areas, and one of her programs reduced the amount of water it took to produce a liter of Pepsi from two and a half liters to one and a half liters. Under her leadership, PepsiCo also, played a pivotal role in the Healthy Weight Commitment Foundation (HWCF), a coalition of sixteen major US food and beverage companies. In 2010, HWCF pledged to eliminate 1.5 trillion calories from the US marketplace by 2015, and just two years later it had eliminated 6.4 *trillion* calories.

Like Polman, Nooyi was able to grow her business beyond market expectations by bringing her beliefs, her purpose, and her identity to work with her. Without clarity about who she was and what she wanted and the commitment to *communicating* what she wanted, she wouldn't have achieved the success she did. She changed how the whole company, including the shareholders, saw PepsiCo. It had become a company with a higher calling than the bottom line, a company that genuinely cared about consumers and all the systems in which they were involved. It was the perfect illustration of what Marx Planck said: "Change the way you look at things, and things you look at will change."

Nooyi's PwP process transcended traditional business models. She envisioned PepsiCo as a workplace that fostered a sense of purpose and belonging for its employees, believing this would naturally lead to increased retention and attract top talent. She recognized that framing success solely through financial metrics doesn't inspire people. Instead, she emphasized the connection between purpose and performance. Her core message was a "virtuous circle": strong performance allows investment in purpose, and a strong sense of purpose fuels outstanding performance. This innovative approach aimed to engage employees on an emotional level, creating a win-win situation for both the company and its workforce.

In the past, it was the badasses who got all the praise in the business world, the ones who epitomized the concept of dog-eat-dog. But Polman and Nooyi introduced the idea that doing good is good business and that caring for people is the best way to transform an organization, even if it employs a hundred thousand people or more. And they did it by living the five pillars.

They identified their integrality: They asked, *Who are the players in my life—my stakeholders?* And besides their literal stakeholders, their lists included the planet, humanity, and society. They saw the systems as whole. And it started with personal perspectives on life—their interests extended far beyond their *own* interests.

They were sure of their intentionality: They asked, *What are my past stories, and how do I reframe them to fit my purpose?* Both worked in companies that had done some harm to society, but they didn't base their communication on defending themselves or apologizing. They just wanted to do things differently and use their companies to affect society positively, and *that's* what they communicated.

They built coherence with the right message: They created missions and strategies to deliver their intentionality to all their stakeholders and the world. And as they spread their messages, more stakeholders joined the cause. Every stakeholder who knew what Polman and Nooyi were working on and why could expand the circle of cooperation, and collaboration could include any new system or stakeholder.

Their companies became lifelong learners: The companies knew their north stars, and because they had a vision that extended beyond the short term and shareholders' return, their integrality grew for their own benefit and they remained clear about their intentionality.

Their companies nurtured transparency: Both developed their own language to communicate the culture and the beliefs they wanted to instill. They fostered environments where open communication was safe and people felt encouraged to share ideas, allowing creativity to flow naturally. When transparency is nurtured and vulnerability is embraced as a strength, deeper human connections are formed. This, in turn, cultivates greater dynamism, flexibility, and the capacity to adapt to change and continuously identify new opportunities.

What impresses me most about Nooyi is her unwavering commitment to authenticity. Besides standing up to criticism for her leadership style, she embraced her femininity in a position dominated by men. When questioned about her use of words like *cherish* and *replenish* when referring to her strategy, which some perceived as overly feminine, she asserted the importance of using language that feels genuine even if it challenges expectations. This approach highlights a crucial aspect of leadership for anyone embarking on transformative initiatives. Skepticism will arise, but a clear vision and unwavering conviction will eventually win over those who truly align with your goals. At the same time, those who are resistant to change may naturally leave the organization, leaving behind a team that's that much more unified and focused on achieving the shared vision.

Living an authentic life starts with uncovering your genuine self, a process that will make a difference in the lives of others, in the systems you belong to, and in the legacy you leave. It's essential to get your why in front of you and know how to communicate it in both your personal and professional spheres. This type of transparency will demonstrate the behavior of an inspiring leader.

When people like Polman and Nooyi spread what they've learned, they bring transparency to the world—transparency about who and what they are and how they do things. They may not have focused on elevating their people's consciousness, but they did! Because they'd acquired the right tools, they elevated their people's awareness about their own lives and empowered them to make an impact in the world through their work.

Transparency is as critical in group and community settings as the four pillars of integrality, intentionality, coherence, and lifelong learning, and that's why the WorkCoherence model considers it an honorary fifth pillar. With transparency in place, a team can enter into resonance—the members understand how each person is carrying out his or her own purpose in alignment with the company's—and work coherently, with all members doing their best because they're working for something more than their paycheck.

Polman and Nooyi wouldn't have succeeded in transforming their companies if they hadn't shared the reasons they were doing what they were doing. By sharing their values and belief systems and explaining the *why* of everything they did—not just to "defend" their actions but also for teaching purposes—they fostered a culture of openness and respect for different beliefs, and it extended to employees, suppliers, clients, and governments around the world. They clearly articulated their purpose and explained their actions and decisions, ensuring that everyone understood their vision. There was coherence in what they were, what they communicated, and how they led their organizations and their lives.

Bringing transparency and vulnerability to any organization is essential—as essential as it is in our daily lives. And the process is the same in families as it is in organizations:

Make your intentions clear. Clearly communicate the intentionality behind decisions and actions.

Share the fact you're talking about (and *stick* to the fact—don't personalize it).

Share your thoughts and feelings about the fact clearly—don't let your emotions speak for you.

Share what you think the best outcome would be.

Instead of this: "I'm your father. You have to trust that I want the best for you. You don't need to know why I'm angry, just that you did wrong and are grounded."

Say this: "I'm your father. I'm doing my best to be a good father, and (not *but*) when I see your decisions and actions, I feel I'm failing at my task as a father. I counted on you to make decisions that would make you happier and more at peace with yourself. Now, as part of educating you, I have to ground you, although I'd rather be having a much more pleasant conversation. What do you think about this?"

Everything changes when we talk about our intentions and motivations, when we explain our fears and show that we decided to act with love. This is the strength of vulnerability and transparency in living our intentions and purpose, living a coherent life.

Vulnerability and transparency also serve organizations, where building trust is essential. How an organization communicates will be crucial for its evolution. And just like in communicating with our families, there are some strategies that are more effective than others. Consider these two approaches that an employee might take to the same issue:

- "Sorry, I can't come to work tomorrow. I have a private thing I need to do."
- "Sorry, I can't come to work tomorrow. I have to sign my divorce papers and I'm going through a hard time. But I love my job and I won't let this get in the way of my work."

In the first example, the employer has lots of room to imagine what the "private thing" is and wonder if the employee is trustworthy. In the second example, the employee expresses his vulnerability, and the employer will probably find no reason not to trust him.

This kind of transparency might not feel natural at first, but it gets easier with practice. The more you practice a new skill or approach, the more pathways and connections you create among brain cells. It's like planting seeds and nurturing them into strong plants. And by using a clear intention and developing the skill or approach, we make our new neuropathways stronger and easier to access. In other words, we strengthen our brain's neuroplasticity, and that's key to creating habits necessary to transforming our behavior to keep up with changes in world dynamics.

Transformations like those that Polman and Nooyi achieved started years before, with the way their environments and the people around them influenced them and with the decisions they made about how to live. Ultimately, they took charge of their lives and framed them to fit their purposes and their values. In other words, they chose a coherent life.

COHERENCE MODEL

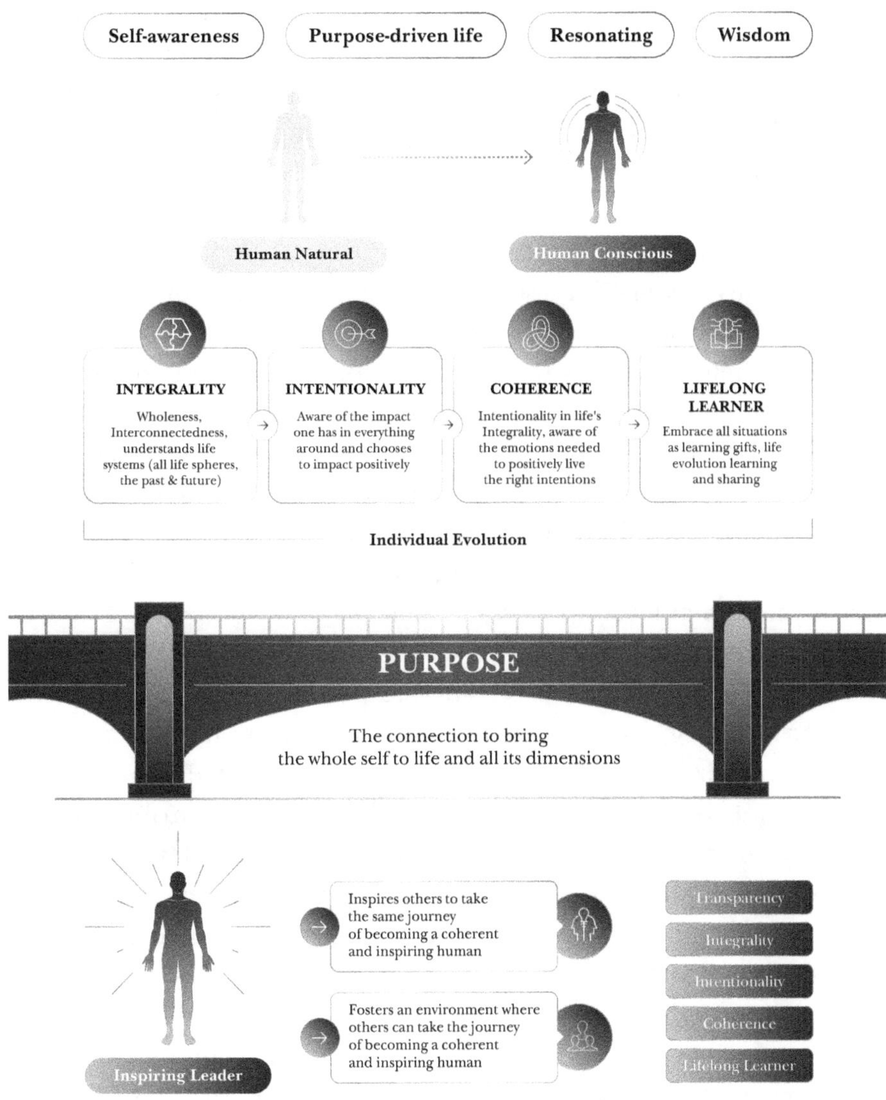

Figure 19

Inspiring Leaders Cultivate Coherence

When an organization has the privilege of being led by someone like Polman who brings transparency and clarity of purpose to the workplace, the level of coherence of the organization is notable. This is where the magic happens. Leaders who cultivate coherence improve the environment, and everyone has a place to grow as human beings, living their purposes and evolving together with the company and its leaders. As a result, productivity happens in a much more sustainable way than when employees work only for the paycheck or under the pressure of radically efficient and finance-focused leadership.

Many consider this an unrealistic and even utopian expectation because many leaders don't walk their talk. When the company's boss claims to be people-focused but sets all goals in terms of financial returns as their seniors, boards, and investors demand, people actually come second and the boss is perceived as deceitful. Parents who want their children to be good human beings send a mixed message when they pressure their children to get into Ivy League schools or at least better schools than the neighbors' kids. Likewise when a spouse says they want their partner to be happy, but only if they make *them* happy first—conditional love. To walk our talk, we have to be very aware of who we are and the impact of our actions.

No matter the setting, a considerate person who walks their talk about prioritizing a group's well-being is a powerful force. They help others recognize their shared visions and the potential for collective achievement. By highlighting the group's ability to contribute something to the society or country they live in, a leader fosters a sense of purpose and collaboration, ultimately drawing out the best in everyone. This focus on coherence, where individual goals align with the team's purpose, is key to building a truly connected and successful unit. And a truly connected unit is something to behold. As the team members work together and witness the positive impact of their combined efforts, their collaboration naturally strengthens, and this virtuous circle of collaboration and individual growth inspires everyone, leading them to build something truly remarkable, something that far exceeds the sum of their individual achievements. And it all starts with a leader who inspires the team to live and work in coherence with their purposes.

When we live a coherent life, we consider others and understand that the outcome we dream of depends on the systems around us. When a star team member works only for personal recognition, making no effort to empower their coworkers, the team's objective may go unmet. But if the star understands that for them to be truly valued and recognized, the objective has to be achieved, they'll use their potential to help others grow so that they *can* achieve it and collectively deliver a great result. Only if success is achieved can an individual be valued as a force for good and an important member of an effective team.

When we understand this, we start to communicate what we're doing, why we're doing it, and why we aren't doing something else. When that's the case, people start to look up to us just like they looked up to Polman and Nooyi. As the graphic below shows, when individuals grow and inspire through their purpose and aligned behavior and transparent communication, they'll have the responsibility to pass this on to their teams, sow the seeds of leadership in others, and create a prosperous, collaborative, and productive culture where everyone is a leader.

COHERENCE MODEL

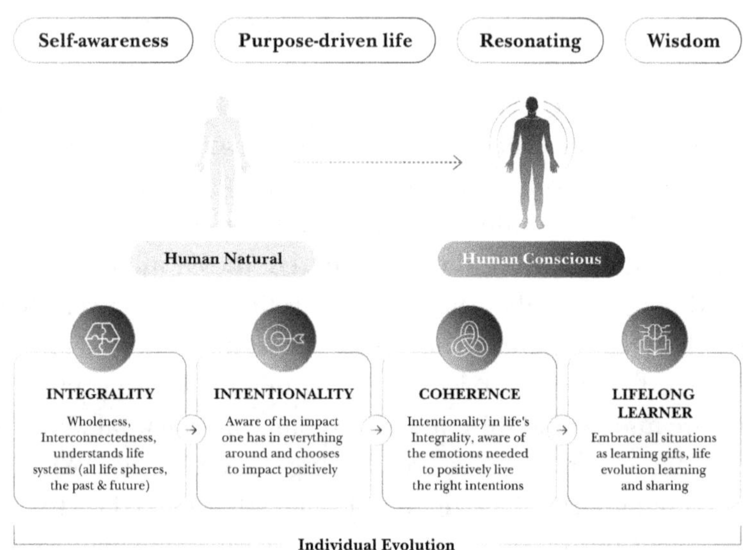

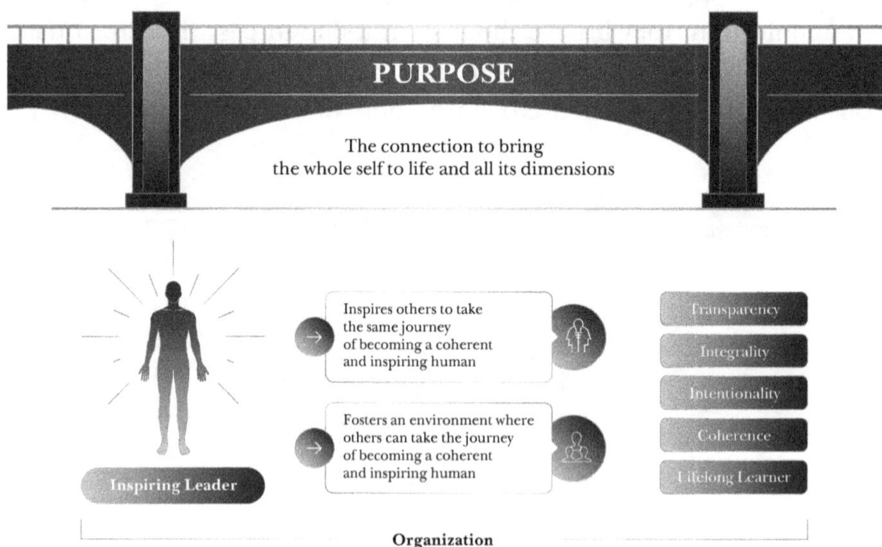

Figure 20

Coherence Raises the World's Consciousness

As more and more of us understand our impact in our environments and live more consciously with the intention to become better human beings and help others transform their lives, the more we raise the consciousness of the world. I used to ask myself what was needed to get us to the next level, what was standing in our way. Now I understand that nobody prevents us from doing it; it's already happening. Consciousness is understanding how to play life's game. Living consciously means getting in there and mixing it up instead of just watching from the sidelines. It means truly *living*.

We often experience a sense of cause and effect in our lives. When we take harmful actions, we may face negative consequences, either immediately or in the future. Conversely, when we perform good deeds, we may experience positive consequences. As we become more aware of what impacts us and how we influence the environment around us and we become more discerning, our consciousness expands and we can be even more discerning. We perceive the consequences of our decisions more accurately, and we're better able to make decisions that align with the path we want to take.

By aligning his decisions with his purpose, Paul Polman raised the consciousness of Unilever's staff. And as a result, he created a culture of coherence. In the next chapter, we'll see how to support this kind of movement toward a world where we can all be true to ourselves *and* serve each other.

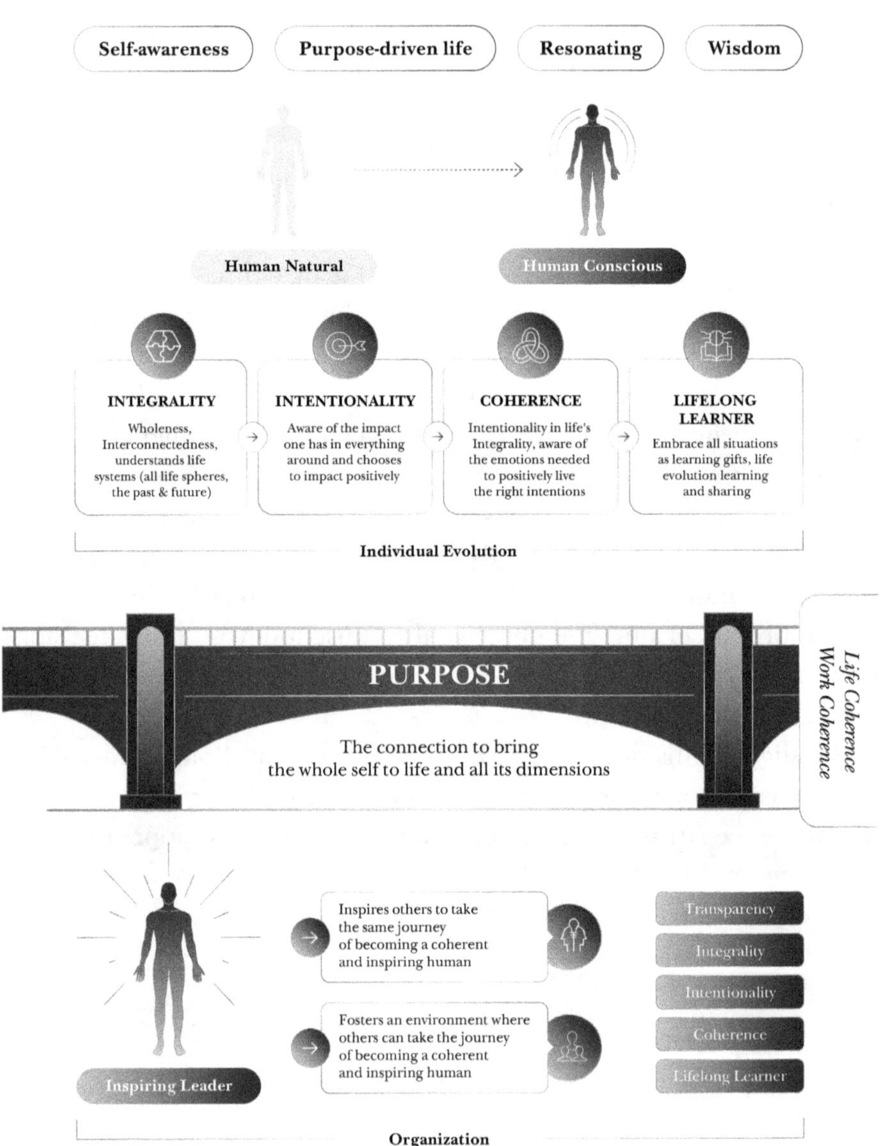
COHERENCE MODEL
Self-awareness
Purpose-driven life
Resonating
Wisdom
Human Natural
Human Conscious
INTEGRALITY
Wholeness, Interconnectedness, understands life systems (all life spheres, the past & future)
INTENTIONALITY
Aware of the impact one has in everything around and chooses to impact positively
COHERENCE
Intentionality in life's Integrality, aware of the emotions needed to positively live the right intentions
LIFELONG LEARNER
Embrace all situations as learning gifts, life evolution learning and sharing
Individual Evolution
PURPOSE
The connection to bring the whole self to life and all its dimensions
Life Coherence
Work Coherence
Inspiring Leader
Inspires others to take the same journey of becoming a coherent and inspiring human
Fosters an environment where others can take the journey of becoming a coherent and inspiring human
Transparency
Integrality
Intentionality
Coherence
Lifelong Learner
Organization

Figure 21

CHAPTER 11

WE SHAPE THE WORLD

During my time in Hungary at the beginning of my leadership journey, I was searching for a balance between the advice I read in business-leadership books and my instincts, the way I was raised. A thirty-two-year-old Brazilian girl on a leadership team with people more than twenty years older than me, I was the youngest and least experienced in the Hungarian market. While unethical competitors were financially incentivizing the medical doctors for prescriptions, my task was to implement a much more ethical work policy within my company. I was offered an executive coach to support me, and she guided me to look for answers inside myself, trust my instincts, and enhance my self-confidence. She was the person who made me understand that embracing who I am is perfectly okay for my professional life.

So that's what I did, sharing my beliefs and learnings with the leaders. In a meeting with the leadership team where we discussed how to prepare the teams to change the way they worked, I pulled out my go-to phrase: "Cowards and heroes both have fears. The difference is that heroes make decisions based on their dreams." And it turned out that what inspired me to face my fears also inspired them. They started to share their knowledge with me, suggesting ways that we could operate more efficiently, train the team in different approaches, and take more responsibility for our work and our impact on society.

Over time, the same things that were happening within the company started happening outside the company. Connections in other parts of my life helped me to live and work the way I believed and to face challenges at work. I even took on the responsibility of creating an ethical code for local and foreign pharma companies on behalf of the Association of International Pharmaceutical Manufacturers. That way we could regulate ourselves instead of waiting for the government to regulate us. I was influencing the environments around me in a way that both served my purpose and greatly benefited *them.* Aligned by a collective vision, we were resonating, and the results were always magic.

What had started as the lonely journey of a person trying to lead a massive transformation of her company through trials and errors of a young believer became a collaborative movement to transform people and an industry sector. Maybe because I was young, maybe because I didn't have all answers, maybe because I saw people who knew much more than I did, or maybe because I believed in people, I ended up creating relationships that helped me build an environment where the future we wanted would have a chance to unfold.

After leaving Hungary, I found that leading a happy, emotionally aware, and purposeful team was much easier with each new leadership position I took. At each company, I started by finding like-minded people who believed in inspiring others to do the right thing and creating a purposeful workplace. That allowed me to establish an environment where I wasn't alone and could make a scalable transformation around me that fostered a future that would work in my favor. I was implementing the integrality principle and intentionality, and a coherence flow like the one in the illustration below was being created.

When you have clarity about your purpose and what you want in life, it can be a very lonely ride, but it doesn't have to be. More people than we imagine want to live a more purposeful, meaningful life too, and when you explicitly share what you're doing and why, the collaborations and alliances will fall into place.

With Neuroplasticity and Epigenetics, We Can Change the World

When it comes to expanding the coherence movement, science is on our side. Thanks to the brain's neuroplasticity, once someone's onboard, their brain is rewired to create the habits they need to develop to achieve the purposeful life they want. But neuroplasticity also has its dangers, making us susceptible to the influence of *in*coherent leaders. On one hand, leaders can create experiences that allow their people to unleash their potential, resulting in an increasingly coherent world. But on the other, they can create experiences that lead to burnout—the corporate disease of this century—and an increasingly sick society.

This power to "rewire" society has to be employed with wisdom. Bosses, parents, and teachers are all human beings and, generally speaking, don't want to harm anyone, but the problem lies in the misguided belief that we have to focus on outputs rather than outcomes—on sales and profitability, good grades, and getting our kids into prestigious colleges rather than on helping our people become good human beings who will make the right decisions and excel, unleashing their exponential potential. If they've developed their skills of discernment and make the most out of themselves, the profitability and the grades and the colleges will be just a few of the rewards they'll enjoy as they evolve.

The fields of psychology and psychiatry have used the powers of neuroplasticity to alter neural connections in ways that support the creation of beliefs and habits that fight addiction and foster healing from emotional trauma, and it works the same way with helping others live coherently. By helping them understand how they can evolve by living a life that's integral, intentional, coherent, and filled with learning, we can free them from living a passive life filled with suffering and regrets. It's a big responsibility.

Fortunately, it's science to the rescue again—we also have epigenetics on our side. This new field of science tells us that certain situations and environments can change our gene expression and have a lifelong impact on our bodies. This means we have the power to create an environment—including our mental environment, our thoughts—that can help us change our bodies and gene expressions to carry the imprint of living a purposeful life further. And building the right environment for those we're caring for will help transform *them.*

In Chapter 6 we mentioned the work of Dr. Bruce Lipton, a firm believer that the power of our thoughts and behavior is one of the main tools of epigenetics. In *The Biology of Belief*, Lipton defends the thesis that how we raise our children will affect their future more than the genes they inherit from us will. Over time, children and their adoptive parents, long-term partners, and long-term colleagues become alike, sometimes even physically. If we know this, we also know we can *trigger* these changes. And the ripple effect this could cause would have an incredibly positive impact on the world. As shown in the graphic below, when the language and behavior of people who live their purpose and their beliefs inspire others, we can observe the ripple effect among families, friends, communities, and business organizations.

Some systems, such as companies, may include large groups of people living their purposes, which makes it easier for those living and talking about purpose. Meanwhile, other systems (represented with red stars in the graphic below) may include very few people living their purposes, with competitive environments driven by financial results, and they may feel too isolated to talk about it. Granted, in order to be heard they would need to talk louder than they would somewhere else, but the effort would bring priceless rewards. In corporate settings where I was alone in my ideas and beliefs, I spoke strongly and openly about my purpose, and some people who hadn't shared their purposes before started to talk about them, and the ripple effect was officially underway. We weren't lonely or isolated in living our purposes anymore!

The secret to touching off a ripple effect is communicating our purposes clearly. When we do this, we influence the systems around us, and the people supporting us will create a network of kindred spirits who want to live a better life and create better environments. That's how movements start. One person can inspire others to find their purposes, and they can align and connect those purposes, build common visions, and create an ever-expanding network, as shown in the graphic below. By working together with aligned purposes, they will realize outcomes that are far greater than what their individual efforts could accomplish.

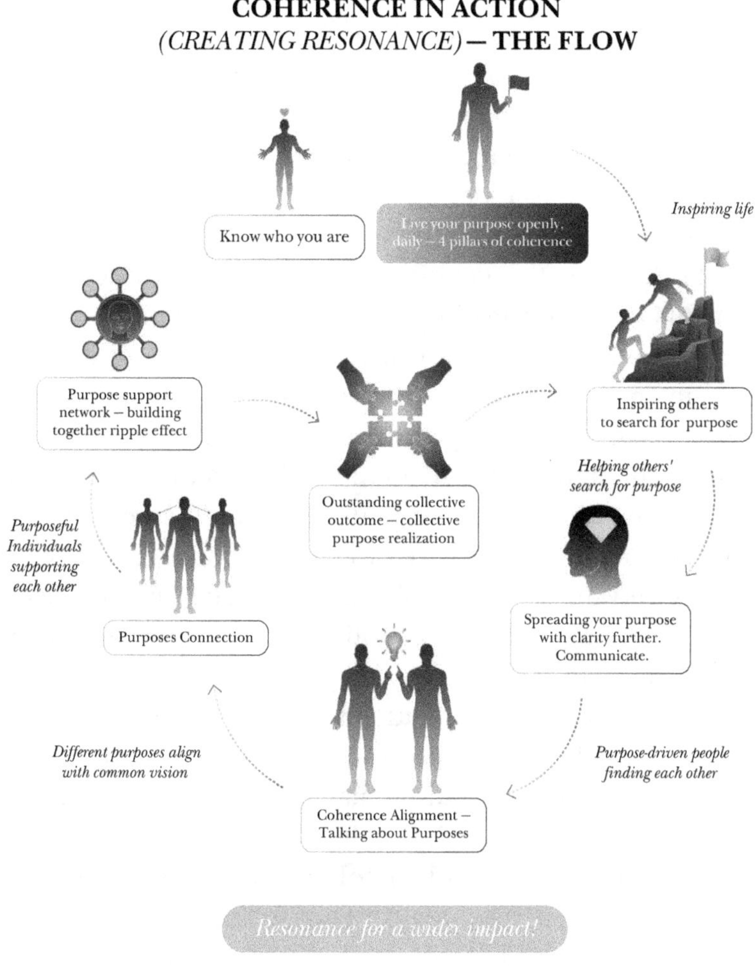

Figure 22

The World's Change Agents Are Consciously Coherent Leaders, Living Purposeful Lives

Everybody who lives a coherent life will become an inspiring leader. It isn't a choice. Humanity has always looked up to examples of people who achieved their dreams and created their futures. When we know we inspire others, we need to help them through their transformations, guiding them and providing an environment where they can thrive. Being conscious of this responsibility as a coherent leader will make life move more efficiently; the more people we help through this journey, the easier our lives will be because more people will understand our lifestyle and help us fulfill our purpose.

These leaders are the genuinely coherent leaders. These leaders are agents of transformation not because they set out to be, but because coherence radiates and inevitably influences others. Their intentionality in all areas of life allows them to model a new way of being: grounded, emotionally attuned, and guided by purpose. As they speak openly about what drives them, their decisions and actions become more conscious and consistent. Over time, their environments begin to shift too, and a network of coherence emerges. These are the leaders who will rise in complex, fast-changing markets because they model the human qualities organizations urgently need. They're the CEOs of the future, able to make fast and meaningful decisions and inspire resilience through authenticity. In contrast, leaders who compartmentalize their lives or live disconnected from their values may gain power temporarily but ultimately lack the trust, clarity, and coherence needed to build enduring human-centered organizations.

We've seen what happens when coherence is lacking. In 2025, a video depicting Andy Byron, then CEO of Astronomer, dancing intimately with the company's global chief HR officer during a Coldplay concert at a leadership event in Foxborough, MA went viral on social media. The footage triggered widespread backlash, raising questions about how leaders represent themselves when they believe they aren't being observed. Even if this was a private moment, eventually not supposed to become public, it did, and many employees and the public saw a disconnect between the company's leadership image and the behavior displayed. It wasn't the dancing itself that caused discomfort—it was the lack of coherence between private conduct and the public expectations of leadership.

In today's world of transparency and hyperconnectivity, leaders can no longer afford to separate their personal values from their professional roles. People want leaders who live integrated lives, whose actions match their words and who lead with humility and emotional maturity across all contexts. Coherent leadership isn't about being perfect; it's about being aligned, consistent, and conscious. The leaders who will thrive in the dynamic markets of the future are those who live authentically, speak openly about their purpose, and inspire trust through the integrity of their daily choices.

As a CEO, I used to try to hire conscious people who knew or were in pursuit of their purposes and wanted to live coherent lives. These are the people we want to have in higher positions. Their ability to make decisions and solve problems is based on a higher level of consciousness and awareness, so the probability of successful solutions and sustainable outcomes that consider society and the bigger picture is higher than with less conscious leaders. The higher the consciousness level, the greater the cognitive maturity of our people and our organization.

But we're living in a transition phase when many professionals still look at work as only the financial part of their lives. To live coherence in the corporate world and nurture it, we need to be open and practice unconditional positive regard. When we can live in a state of unconditional acceptance, we're able to see the infinite opportunities instead of living within the limitations created by our doubts and criticism of others who aren't living in coherence.

As agents of change, although we may rather build our companies with highly conscious people, we have the responsibility to create the right environment for those of lower consciousness to become more conscious. And it's good for us—leading and living in diversity is a chance to learn and grow from it, and it's when agents of change are at their most inspiring. Examples are set when tough decisions have to be made.

In one of the guided meditations I practice to expand my consciousness, a Buddhist monk says, "I ask the universe to send me gifts for me to grow and training situations where I can test and improve them." How brilliant—we'll only be able to grow and to develop gifts like patience and love if we're tested. It's in the moments of confronting differences among thoughts and perspectives that we know ourselves. These are the moments when we have to sit back and ask again: *What is the integrality of my life? And is there anything new to include in my beliefs?*

To guide your reflections, you might also ask yourself:

- What were my intentions?
- Why did I have these intentions?
- What was my ultimate purpose?
- What do I really want, and how can this moment train me to live what I believe?
- What do I have to have clarity about?

Consciously Coherent Leaders Impact Their Systems

All communities and organizations—churches, HOAs, activist groups, political parties, corporations—are hungry for real leadership, and when coherent leaders arrive on the scene, they make a huge difference. Being leaders means we'll significantly impact others, and maybe without our even knowing it, our ideas, thoughts, and beliefs will form new neural connections in people's brains and change the way they think. Even if you're only with them for a short time, your way of living can have a strong effect on them.

The question is how to influence them the way you *want* to influence them. It's important to observe the communication and behavior you use to represent the four parts of the coherence journey that define us and understand how they affect the systems around us:

Integrality

Past Relationships
How have your relationships helped with your purpose journey?

How do they affect the systems around you?

Environment

How have your environments helped with your purpose journey?
How do they affect how you behave in the different systems around you?

Future Relationships

How do your relationships and their likely effect on the future help with your purpose journey?
Are these relationships the ideal relationships to build the systems around you as you envision them? How can you align them?

Environment

How do your environments and their likely effect on the future help with your purpose journey?
Are you in the right environment to live the system change you're dreaming of?

Intentionality

Missions in different environments/relationships
Why do you do what you do in the various circles of your life?
How do you select your environments/relationships?

Coherence

How do you live the same life with the same purpose in all the relationships and environments of your life?
How do you ensure that your motivations (emotions) align with your intentions (thoughts) so that your actions represent those intentions?

Lifelong learning

How do you align all your intentionality in all the systems that enter your life to maintain coherence?
How do you pass your learnings on to others?
Now let's look at your role in the various systems you navigate and how you can bring coherent leadership to each one:

Friends

When you're among friends, be the inspiring one who brings positive energy. Talk about the good you can achieve wherever you are. And observe the energies among your friends. There are different ways to live and to appreciate life, and you can observe which energies can serve your purpose and which can't. Choosing to be part of what serves your purpose helps you grow as a human being. One of the rewards of being with friends is that we can elevate each other's consciousness this way.

As for the effect your friends have on you, the environment they create will influence you to be at your best or *not* your best, and you might make snap decisions that can make your journey to what you want to be either harder or easier. Remember the story of the Brazilian congressman and the "innocent" text he sent to his friends' WhatsApp group about the Ukrainian women? Always keep in mind that no matter whether your intentions are serious or foolish, what you do with friends will have consequences that will be part of your life forever.

So choose your friends well. And use them as a training ground for becoming more intentional about what you want and working on your awareness of how your language and behavior are shaping who you are.

Relationships

In a relationship, for you to be able to influence your partner positively, to bring out the best in him or her, you have to understand how your partner's thoughts and behaviors are affecting you. When we're in a love relationship, we tend to adapt to be accepted; we change according to our partner's language and behavior in order to build rapport. But maintaining clarity about who we are and what we want for our future as a human being will help the relationship evolve to higher levels of consciousness.

There's power in being intentional about our relationships and living our purpose together. When we do that, we can have a greater positive impact on the people and environment around us than we can have as individuals. Our love relationships can be a great space to learn about ourselves and how we can bring out the best in others. Talk openly about what you'd both like to get from the relationship. How are you and your partner influencing people and environments when you're together? How are your friends affecting you or your relationship, and how are you influencing your friends? In what new ways could you and your partner affect each other positively? Can you keep transforming your relationship by consciously building and scaling what you both want?

Creating good communication and behavior habits while becoming more coherent human beings—and leaders—is easier done together than alone. And it's not just your relationship that will be the better for it. Thanks to the ripple effect, the *world* will be better for it.

Families

There's a significant benefit in having a whole-family purpose. It's at home that our language and behavior have the biggest effect on others' brains, and the earlier we start the journey of coherence the better. By living a coherent life within the family, we build a foundation for knowing who we are and allow ourselves a place to experiment with what living coherently can mean. Most of the time, family members will express themselves more honestly when this is the case than they otherwise would.

Conflict is also minimized when there's an alignment of values and purpose in a family. Often, family discussions end up being about who's right or wrong and who will give in to the other's way of thinking, but things are different when there's clarity about what the family wants to bring forward. We can start with small things like wanting to be a family that performs kind acts (volunteering, for example) and creates good feelings wherever we are, and as we continue to live that purpose as our children grow up, who's "right" in family discussions will matter less and less. What will matter more and more is whether we're achieving our purpose at any given time. If the answer is no, the discussion will be about how to achieve it.

Parents can also guide a family's running discussion by saying, "We want you to learn to make the right decisions and be responsible for the consequences of your choices." When both parents repeat this phrase, an alignment will happen, and a value of responsibility and a purpose of doing good will be implicit. And you'll be modeling how you want your family to use language. After all, as everybody knows, children won't do what we tell them to do, but they *will* mirror our behavior. If we want them to talk about their school experiences or other life experiences, we can share our own experiences and vulnerabilities to create a safe and open environment where they feel comfortable doing the same.

Modeling at home coherence and explaining our intentions to be good parents will set an example of transparent communication. The more we talk about intentions and motivations and express our emotions in words instead of simply reacting, the more aware of their own intentions and motivations our children will be, and expressing their emotions will be that much easier. In other words, by providing coherent guidance within our families, we'll be making our children's adolescence significantly easier—a big step toward a more harmonious, coherent world.

Organizations

For years, the definition of a good executive, businessperson, or professional was someone who could completely separate their emotions from their work and always be rational—a machine that never fails, always better than others and never bringing personal matters to work.

To be "grown-up" at work meant building a persona different from what the vast majority of us really are or would want to be.

When you become part of a group in a corporation or other business, the existing culture will influence you. For many people, this is the area where it's trickiest to be ourselves. Most of us will be concerned with how we're perceived, how we'll have to *act* to be seen that way, and this will create neural connections that change the way we think (remember neuroplasticity?). The further we get from our essence, the harder it is to be productive and have the impact we want. And with time we won't even recognize who we are.

On the other hand, when we know our purpose and the person we want to be, we can fit a new work environment into our purpose and frame it according to our needs. The outcome of our work will be more impactful than the outcome for those who are trying to change who they are in order to adapt to the environment. People with clarity about who they are *shape* the environment according to what they see in their future. And then these inspiring leaders will either grow in their work or, if the organization doesn't have the environment to allow them to prosper while being themselves, look for a place where they *can*.

Leaders can build an environment where people with clarity about who they are can find their purposes and inspire others. These are the people we want to have working with us. In organizations where they can thrive, there will be less burnout, depression, and other health problems than at organizations where people need to wear masks. Finding kindred spirits at work and living a coherent life can make a huge difference in our future, and coherent leaders and teams who foster these environments will have a positive impact on the world that's more powerful than what they could achieve on their own. Businesses and organizations are nothing more than the culture their people form—the more nurturing the culture, the more sustainable the prosperity and legacy they'll build.

Coherent Organizations Generate Systemic Prosperity

In the same way that leaders impact their teams, organizations impact society. Apple, for example, has changed how humanity thinks. Because of Apple, our neuroplastic brains had to create new neural connections to listen to music, watch videos, and talk to each other on a single device. At the same time, it led other companies to focus more on the future and to be more innovative and creative. This example of collective neuroplasticity is a transformation that can never be turned back.

Apple could only do this because it had behaved coherently through the years. The collective intellect it built among coworkers that made it possible to bring such innovative products to market was the result of a bold vision founded on a strong purpose that still resonates throughout the organization until today. That's why jobs with Apple are so sought-after and its products are must-haves.

Another corporate example of coherence at a high service level is Patagonia. In 2022, company founder Yvon Chouinard announced that he and his family were literally giving the company away. According to the *New York Times*:

> *Mr. Chouinard, his wife and two adult children have transferred their ownership of Patagonia, valued at about $3 billion, to a specially designed trust and a nonprofit organization. They were created to preserve the company's independence and ensure that all of its profits—some $100 million a year—are used to combat climate change and protect undeveloped land around the globe.*

It would be hard to find a more vivid and inspiring example of coherence in action than what Chouinard and Patagonia have achieved. Patagonia's decisions reflect a profound alignment with the pillars of the WorkCoherence model we've explored throughout this book:

Integrality: Patagonia honors the interconnectedness of all systems: environment, society, customers, employees, and future generations.

Every decision considers the impact on all stakeholders, not just shareholders, embracing the reality that we exist within, not apart from, the ecosystems we inhabit.

Intentionality: The company's clear, unwavering purpose—to save the planet—isn't just a slogan; it's the guiding force behind every strategic and operational choice. Patagonia invites others to join this movement, making purpose a shared societal mission rather than an isolated corporate goal.

Coherence: Patagonia's values aren't just written on websites or brochures; they're embedded in actions, products, governance, and culture. Purpose and behavior are consistently aligned, creating a living model of coherence across all relationships and decisions.

Lifelong learning: Recognizing that the world is dynamic and complex, Patagonia continuously adapts. Its shift from maximizing profits to dedicating profits to climate action shows an openness to evolve, to learn from emerging realities, and to act with courage and creativity.

Transparency: From its environmental impact reports to the unprecedented transfer of ownership to a trust and nonprofit, Patagonia remains radically open about what it stands for, how it operates, and where it believes its responsibility lies. Transparency is part of its very essence.

By structuring its existence around these pillars, Patagonia shows that living and leading coherently is possible. The Chouinard family's lifestyle reflects an alignment of personal values and actions. And the company's success serves as a powerful reminder that when we align our beliefs, intentions, and actions with the systems we're part of, we can achieve personal well-being *and* make a positive impact on the planet, contributing to the regeneration of life itself.

But it's important to remember that we aren't all Yvon Chouinard and we aren't all working for Patagonia. And that's perfectly okay. His example is a first courageous step that shows us a path. Each of us, wherever we are—whether leading a company, building a career inside a traditional organization, or even rethinking our personal choices—can take steps toward greater coherence.

Coherence isn't reserved for the few who make headlines. It belongs to each of us, in the choices we make, in the culture we build around us, and in the silent yet powerful example we set. Every small act of aligning our values with our actions helps to change the systems we're part of, and when we live this way, we contribute to a deeper transformation where success is measured by our positive impact on the lives we touch, the communities we strengthen, and the future we help create. Even the smallest step, when taken with purpose, makes us proud architects of a more coherent world.

A More Coherent World Is Unfolding

Despite the chaos inherited from previous generations—corporate burnout, species extinction, climate change, rising depression, technology-driven isolation—there's growing evidence that the seeds of coherence we're planting today are beginning to blossom. Consider some signs of progress, reported by organizations like the United Nations, UNESCO, NASA, and the World Health Organization:

- The global extreme poverty rate has fallen dramatically, from nearly 36 percent in 1990 to less than 9 percent today.
- Global child mortality rates have been cut by more than half since 1990.
- Renewable energy capacity worldwide has tripled over the past decade.
- Youth literacy rates now exceed 91 percent globally.
- Species such as the humpback whale, the bald eagle, and the giant panda have rebounded from near extinction thanks to global conservation efforts.

These victories tell a story: When people act with clarity, coherence, and compassion, change happens—both at a systemic and a planetary level. But the transformation isn't happening only in governments and ecosystems. It's also taking root inside businesses, communities, and the ways we work together every day. Across the globe, companies are beginning to embrace new ways of working that foster human flourishing and long-term sustainability:

- **Buurtzorg (Netherlands),** a pioneering healthcare organization built on self-managed teams and trust-based leadership, is achieving both exceptional patient satisfaction and operational efficiency without rigid hierarchies.
- **Viisi (Netherlands)** is a financial services company fully structured as a Teal organization where employees make decisions collectively and purpose—not profit—is the primary driver.
- **Kin Restaurant (USA)** offers full-time salaried positions with benefits in an industry known for precarious work, achieving high employee retention, customer loyalty, and national acclaim.
- **Atlassian (Australia)** created "Team Anywhere," a global remote work strategy fostering flexibility, innovation, and employee well-being without sacrificing productivity.
- **Nike Europe** has adopted Obeya Rooms to foster rapid collaboration, real-time alignment, and collective decision-making.
- **SAS Institute** built a culture centered on employee well-being—with on-site childcare, healthcare, and fitness centers—and has achieved outstanding employee retention and consistent profitability.
- **Google** empowered innovation with its "20% Time," encouraging employees to pursue passion projects, leading to creations like Gmail and AdSense.

The principles of coherence apply whether we're saving coral reefs, restructuring companies, or simply choosing to lead a meeting with more empathy and clarity. When we exercise integrality, intentionality, coherence, lifelong learning, and transparency, we align our deepest essence with the systems we belong to and build a new future together.

This isn't about perfection. It's about a movement. It's about recognizing that challenges and conflicts aren't the end—they're invitations to grow together, to learn together, and to build a future where humanity and the planet can thrive as one.

The collective neuroplasticity of humanity is awakening. New pathways are being formed—pathways of hope, solutions, compassion, and collaboration. You don't have to be a founder of a global movement. You don't have to change the world overnight. But you can choose to live intentionally today. You can be the leader—within your family, your team, your company, your community—who embodies coherence and inspires others to do the same.

The world is waiting for coherent leaders. Are you ready to be one?

Who will you inspire today?

ACKNOWLEDGMENTS

To everyone who was part of my happy and fulfilling thirty-year executive career: leaders, colleagues, providers, industry peers, fellow association members, embassies, local government authorities, and all the other angels who made my life in seven different countries so special, full of learning, and filled with unforgettable memories. Each of you helped me open up, take the observer's seat in my own life, and learn—about you, about myself, and about how we could bring out the best in each other to make the world a better place. You taught me that it's possible to have a successful professional life and an even more meaningful personal life when we live with purpose.

To Bayer, where I found incredible leaders who believed in a young Brazilian woman of Japanese descent and trusted her with leadership roles in Brazil, Portugal, Hungary, Slovakia, Mexico, and Venezuela. Thank you for opening doors that showed me a world that transformed knowledge into wisdom. Thank you for giving me countless "first times" that expanded my consciousness. You nurtured in me the light of not only having a job but having a purpose. With Bayer, I learned who I was as a human being and who I wanted to be as a professional. Bayer showed me the world and made me a global citizen. I understood that being coherent in life is critical to feeling fulfilled—and because of this, Bayer and all colleagues there will forever be in my heart.

To Roche, who gave me the opportunity to become the professional I'd dreamed of becoming at Bayer and allowed me to bring humanity, spirituality, purpose, and love into leadership. Thank you for welcoming me in Venezuela and sending me to India. In these two countries, I learned to simplify complexity and to see that clarity comes from love, compassion, and purpose. I learned that a leader is someone who helps others become better human beings. Roche taught me that we must live and lead according to our values, dreams, and purpose. And Roche also taught me that our biggest lessons may arrive when we least expect them—but if we embrace them, they transform our knowledge and intellect into wisdom. Lifelong learning is wisdom that allows us to live in plenitude.

To my clients—my friends and partners in crime—with whom I keep learning how to live a better life while becoming a better leader and a better human being. After every workshop, every mentoring session, every speech, *I* learn the most; I feel inspired to bring more consciousness to humanity. The light I see in your eyes when an insight blooms—the humanity and goodness that emerge in that moment—motivates me to keep learning and sharing how loving-kindness and compassion can create a more systemic way of living and working. I hope to witness many more insights and to see many of you spreading compassion and living your purpose.

A deep bow to my masters—Yoga, Hinduism, Vedanta, Kabbalah, Buddhism, and all the teachers and gurus who kept me on the path of spirituality, curiosity, and belief. I continue to be surprised by the wisdom that humanity carries, and the beauty already present among us. Every time I pause to contemplate a new teaching—or an old one—I surrender. I've learned that the secret to a fulfilled life is already here; we just need to listen when we stumble upon it.

To the scientists and philosophers who transformed ancient philosophies into modern science—Fritjof Capra, Bruce Lipton, Otto Scharmer, Daniel Goleman, Joe Dispenza, Richard Davidson, and so many others. Thank you for giving me the language to bring Eastern spirituality to leadership with a "Western accent."

A special "thank you," filled with love, to **Professor Danah Zohar**, whose books my mother gave me long before she became my mentor. She supported and inspired my leadership experiments in India and later introduced me to Taoism and Chinese philosophy. We spent hours exchanging thoughts about the connections between quantum physics and leadership. I'll never be able to thank you enough.

Alzira, you made me stop shying away from calling my insights and thoughts "my model." Every Friday for the last three years, you've reminded me why I must keep doing what I'm doing. You inspire me and push me to my limits, and because of your mission to help others live their purpose and bring it to the world, I now have many projects in the works to serve humanity.

To Toni Robino, you were tireless. You never let me give up on this book. Every time I was about to put it aside, you motivated me. Your book-architecture process is genius, and your purpose inspired me every second of this journey. And when discouragement came again, **Doug Wagner** brought clarity. Doug, you helped make sense of many of my thoughts and masterfully doctored and edited the book, teaching me the art of storytelling. This book exists because of you two.

To Gordon McClellan, from our first call, your story and purpose enchanted me. I saw the magic DartFrog Books uses to turn dreams into reality. It made me want to bring this book to the world faster—with you. Thank you for welcoming me and all my crazy ideas.

To the wonderful crew at Horizon West, Hamlin Starbucks, you made my writing Tuesdays a magical time. For the last two years, you welcomed me with such care, often checking in to see how my book was progressing. **Maureen and Chris**, your warm smiles—especially on the days I stayed more than eight hours—made me feel at home. While I was writing this book about living and working with love and purpose, you inspired me by embodying exactly the kind of workplace and coworker spirit I believe in. You showed me, week after week, what it means to create an environment where people feel seen, valued, and happy to return. I'll keep writing just so I can keep coming back to Starbucks Hamlin every Tuesday!

Dad, your purpose has guided every decision in my life. The way you live your work—with love and devotion—made me want to live with the same passion wherever I am. But above all, your love and your deep belief in me make me always look beyond, because honestly, how could I ever tell you, "I can't"? This book is for you—keep telling your friends about me. ;) I love you. I am your mini-me, and I'm proud of it.

Marcelo and Maya, you are my ground and my soul. Because of you, I learned resilience and learned to stand up after deep falls. No one would be reading this book today if it weren't for Christmas 2006 and all the moments you came to rescue me after Mom died. Knowing you are there always makes my life easier and brighter. Our sibling bond is pure love, and your unconditional teachings live inside this book. Thank you for existing in my life. You are my safe harbor.

Kiño, Sasa, and Lily, what could I ever write to make you understand that I'm in this life for you—and that I wrote this book in hopes of ensuring that you have a bright future and inherit a world where work is a place of pleasure and fulfillment. Because of you, I keep pushing myself to be a better human being, and I keep searching for ways to help others be better human beings too. You deserve to live in a world where your best can shine every day. Thank you for choosing me as your mother.

Régis, I hope I can be half the human being you believe I am. Your belief makes me learn more and be more. You are the reason I deeply trust the words of Max Planck's that I repeat so often: "When you change the way you look at things, the things you look at change." You taught me to see differently. During our 5 a.m. walks, every time I shared an insight, you challenged me, asked deeper questions, and later drew what you saw—until suddenly, *bam*, I understood. You make my mission less frightening. You make me believe I can live my purpose of elevating humanity's consciousness. *Ubuntu* — I am because we are.

Finally, Mom, this book is for you. For the past twenty years, the presence of your absence has been immense. When you were physically here, you taught me to be the person you believed could change the world. After you died, I had to be that person so that you could see, from wherever you are, the world you believed in. I carry a responsibility that wakes up and goes to bed with me every day: I am your legacy, and I love who I am becoming because of this. You made my Dharma easier and my Karma more pleasant. For you, I will keep learning, keep evolving, and keep sharing. Wherever you are, send me your blessings. I feel you—every day.

ABOUT THE AUTHOR

Lara Bezerra's understanding of leadership was shaped long before she entered the corporate world. Raised by parents who were medical doctors, she learned early that work can be an expression of service and responsibility, not merely a means of achievement. Her Japanese mother profoundly influenced her way of thinking, nurturing her natural integration of science, philosophy, and disciplined inner inquiry.

Across a thirty-year executive career, Lara served as CEO and senior leader in multinational organizations such as Bayer and Roche, leading complex businesses in seven countries in Latin America, Europe, and Asia. While serving as CEO in India, she became the world's first chief purpose officer, pioneering the formal integration of purpose into leadership, organizational culture, and strategic decision-making.

Through this journey, Lara came to know that leaders can always choose to shape organizations into nurturing environments where results and organizational well-being are mutually reinforcing, allowing people to realize themselves both professionally and personally.

After leaving corporate life, Lara devoted herself to researching and developing frameworks that help individuals and organizations live and operate coherently in an increasingly complex world. She is the founder of WorkCoherence®, where she advises CEOs, boards, and leadership teams globally on aligning human development, business performance, and societal impact.

A global citizen and mother of three, Lara was born in Brazil and shaped by life across Europe, Asia, and the Americas. Her work sits at the intersection of business, consciousness, and systemic transformation, guiding leaders to build results that are not only successful but meaningful and enduring. She lives in Florida with her husband and their three children.

www.ingramcontent.com/pod-product-compliance
Lightning Source LLC
Chambersburg PA
CBHW051411050726
47595CB00010B/4019

* 9 7 8 1 9 6 5 2 5 3 8 7 8 *